Have a Heavenly Marriage

Have a Heavenly Marriage

By
David H. Sorenson

P. O. Box 1099, Murfreesboro, TN 37133

Printed and Bound in the United States of America

CONTENTS

Section I—Foundational Principles

1. Heaven on Earth—More Than Just a Metaphor 3

2. Psychology, Sociology or Scripture?............................11

3. The Issues of Life Are Fundamentally Spiritual........23

Section II—Building Blocks of a Heavenly Marriage

4. *Agape* Love 41

5. *Phileo* Love 65

6. Righteousness 89

7. Family Finances 101

Section III—Scripture Passages Regarding Marriage

8. An Exposition of Ephesians 5:21–33 127

9. An Exposition of I Peter 3:1–7...............................145

10. An Exposition of I Corinthians 7:1–6.....................163

11. An Exposition of Colossians 3:4–19........................177

Section IV—Final Thoughts

12. The Fundamental Problem and God's Solution 197

13. Putting It All Together 217

SECTION I

FOUNDATIONAL PRINCIPLES

1.

HEAVEN ON EARTH—MORE THAN JUST A METAPHOR

HELL ON EARTH?

As a pastor I have had the opportunity over the years to observe hundreds and hundreds of marriages. A certain percentage of these couples have come for counseling, though most have not. Nevertheless, a pastor learns a lot about what goes on in the families connected with his church.

For some people, marriage is a degree of Hell on earth. They fight, they bicker, they pout, and their homes are often in a state of cold war, occasionally breaking into open battle. They are miserable and frustrated, and marital bliss to them is some kind of cruel joke.

I have witnessed marriages that are one-way streets. It may be *he* or it may be *she* who rules, but one spouse does so with either an iron fist or a brass mouth. If there is not physical fighting, there is verbal warfare.

I've witnessed numerous times the twenty- or thirty-something-year-old husband who has never grown up. He lives for his toys. When he was little, his toys would fit under the Christmas tree. Now he needs an extra garage to house them. There is the four-wheeler, the boat, the snowmobile or jetski™. There are the camper, the canoe and the fishing gear. There are the hunting artillery, the computer stuff and the sports stuff. Oh yes, and there also is the wife, if he has any time left over. He just can't seem to understand why she is always bugging him about spending some time with her. He works lots of overtime to pay for these things. He brings home the bacon and pays the bills. "What's the big deal about my leisure time?"

Perhaps she is the domineering wife who in personality resembles the general's wife in the popular cartoon strip. She's overweight, has a short temper and has a very sharp mouth. She lives for her interests—shopping, craft shows, school affairs, lunch with the girls—and spends money like there is no tomorrow.

Then there is the wife who dreads her husband on payday. He invariably comes home drunk that night. All the frustrations and aggravations from years of bickering are unleashed as the alcohol loosens his better judgment. He berates and belittles her. He shoves her around. He calls her all kinds of vulgar and base names. He shouts at the children and complains that "nobody ever cares about me!" When bedtime finally comes, there is an icy atmosphere that has settled over the house. Everyone is glad the "old man" has finally fallen asleep.

Then there is the spouse who is chagrined, deeply wounded and utterly humiliated to find out his or her mate has been having an affair. The very glues of trust and love which have held their marriage together are strained to the breaking point. There are resentment, frustration and bitterness. There is a deep sense of betrayal and hopelessness. How could he or she have been so unfaithful? Emotions run the gamut from anger and hatred, bordering on the contemplation of murder, to utter despair, considering suicide. Some try to bury it all with drunken forgetfulness.

Also there are numerous homes where one partner or the other has run up the credit card bill, besides the car payment, the rent or the mortgage payment. Add to that insurance bills and utility payments *ad infinitum*, and there is more month than there is money. Consequently, bickering and recriminating statements are fired back and forth. One blames the other. Threatening notices about legal action come in the mail or on the phone, the car is about to be repossessed, and insurance is about to be cancelled. The checking account is empty, and the pressure builds. Each notice or unpleasant phone call only puts more stress and acrimony into the marriage.

Having been in the ministry for more than a quarter of a century, I can recall spouses of both genders coming to me utterly devastated upon learning of their mates' infidelity. I have listened to the tales of woe of family finances stretched beyond the limit. I have heard the ugly stories of spouses of both genders and their drunkenness. I have witnessed the icy, steely glares of couples in the throes of divorce. For more than for those who are willing to admit it, marriage is indeed a taste of Hell on earth.

HEAVEN ON EARTH

God did not intend marriage to be a taste of Hell on earth. There are those whose marriages are a taste of Heaven on earth. I know whereof I speak, for by God's grace my wife and I have a marriage that is that. For us, the idea that marriage can be heaven on earth is more than just a metaphor. It is more than just the proverbial wedded bliss.

In twenty-five years of marriage there has been total, complete fidelity to each other. (Later in this book we will get into the biblical principles that have given us an intense fidelity to each other.) In twenty-five years of marriage, neither of us has ever physically abused the other. There has not been a physical fight. There has not been a shove nor a slap nor even the threat of such. The truth is, over these twenty-five years, I cannot recall a time when we ever shouted at each other or even raised our voices at each other. We not only have been one flesh; we also have been one mind, one emotion and one spirit.

We have always asked the Lord if He were to take either

of us to Heaven, to take us both at the same time. Our lives are so integrally woven together that we are not two people, but one.

There has been an abiding love for each other that has grown through these years. We truly love each other more today than we did the day we were married. We know each other far better. Consequently, we long for each other more. We are a part of each other.

Have there ever been disagreements in our marriage? Indeed. However, if we could rate the intensity of our disagreements on a scale of zero to ten, with zero being no disagreement and ten, vehement fighting, what little fussing we have done would be in the very low digits.

That is not because we are both timid, mousy personalities. We both are somewhat aggressive in setting goals and accomplishing the same. We both attend to full-time professional duties. However, we have learned and integrated biblical precepts and principles that have added a very pleasant tranquility to our marriage.

Our home has been a place of love and trust. It has been a joint venture of working together to serve the Lord in whatever place or capacity we found ourselves. I think in twenty-five years we have lived in at least twelve different places—apartments, rented houses, parsonages and, finally, our own homestead. Wherever we have been, we have had happiness together.

We were one in our days in seminary when I had mononucleosis and Pam had to work to support us. We were one when I was an assistant pastor and Pam was at home with the children. We were one when I was the pastor and she was my secretary. We were one when we started a church and she worked in a law firm to help support the family. We have always been one.

We have been on the same wavelength spiritually, mentally, emotionally and in physical intimacy. Though there have been outside pressures over the years, we always have been unified. We have been a partnership. That partnership has extended throughout our family and home so that even our children have been one with us in serving the Lord.

We have not allowed outside pressures to work their way between us. I am reminded of a funny stunt our most recent Dalmatian dog has tried over the last several years. She is an affectionate dog and seeks to be the center of attention when we are around her. I will sometimes purposely make a point to hug my wife in the dog's presence. We will stand and hug each other and quite audibly say, so the dog can hear, "I love you."

Well, that is more than Lady can bear. She invariably will trot over, jump up, put her front paws up on us and try to "hug" us as well. If she had her "druthers," she would try to get right between us, but we won't let her. That is symbolic of how our marriage has been.

At bedtime if the girls are at home, they will let the dog into our bedroom while we lie there reading, and Lady will flop herself between us trying to lick one or the other of us on the face. She wants to get between us, but she never can.

Our home has been a place of peace, happiness, fulfillment, friendship, fun, working together and romance. There is not going to be romance in Heaven as we would think of it here, but I do think Heaven will in some considerable measure be like our home has been. There will be no fighting or bickering, no sarcasm or name-calling. There will be peace, love, happiness and thoughtfulness. There will be no distrust, anger, hatred or bitterness. There will be no need for forgiveness because there will be no sin. It all will be unified around an eternal desire to serve the Lord and to live for Him forever.

In fact, in Heaven someday there will be a major marriage relationship. It will be between Jesus Christ and the church. The principles which will make that marriage celestial and eternal are outlined and detailed in the Bible. Those same principles can be applied to our marriages today. That is what this book is all about.

I believe God intended our homes and our marriages to be a taste of Heaven on earth. The world around us may be corrupt. Our marriages need not be. There may be all manner of ugliness, bitterness, frustration, distrust and trouble out in the world; but our homes and our marriages need not be characterized by these.

That which has made our marriage a taste of Heaven on earth has not been by accident. It has not been just some lucky coincidence of two people who are completely compatible finding each other and living happily ever after. Rather, our marriage has been patterned after and built upon spiritual and scriptural principles any couple can adopt and integrate into their lives. I shall seek to explain these principles to you so that you also may have a marriage which is heaven on earth.

A principle which will run throughout this book is that the issues of life are fundamentally spiritual. We will develop this concept more fully later. There are few things which could be considered issues of life more than our marriages, our families or our homes. The key to a marriage which is heaven on earth is spiritual. Spiritual principles and practices will profoundly influence the character and tone of a marriage.

It is more than coincidence that the title to this book is *Have a Heavenly Marriage*. God's Heaven is a place to which one may go only through a spiritual relationship to Jesus Christ. It is a place where the most excellent spiritual attributes, such as holiness, righteousness and love, will prevail.

Likewise, a marriage like Heaven on earth will have the spiritual qualities of holiness, righteousness and love.

As the essence of this book unfolds, it will become apparent the secret to a heavenly marriage is for *both* parties to live authentic, spiritual, righteous Christian lives. There are no shortcuts—no such thing as "six easy steps to a blissful marriage." Only genuine biblical Christianity by *both* parties will produce a marriage relationship which can be described as "heaven on earth."

2.
PSYCHOLOGY, SOCIOLOGY OR SCRIPTURE?

America in the late twentieth century has become a land of humanistic philosophy and values. Sadly, this has filtered down into the lives of Christian people. We live in an era which I would characterize as the secularization of America. In my lifetime (I was born in 1946), the prevailing culture of America has become almost completely secular.

The "mystery of iniquity" under the banner of "separation of church and state" has been egged on by the ACLU. It has been aided and abetted by a sympathetic news media and encouraged by eager accomplices in liberal congresses. It has been promoted by activist courts and by "cultural elitists" embedded in most institutions of higher learning. Together they have managed to bring a near total divorce of anything that is even remotely godly from the civic arena. Perhaps this is most pronounced in the public schools of the land. We witness the results of their handiwork in the societal and cultural deterioration of our country.

A FALSE RELIGION

A new religion has arisen in America. Its cathedrals are universities and science laboratories. Its scripture is the *Humanist Manifesto*, related New Age writings and endless "new scientific studies." Its clergy are called psychologists, psychiatrists and sociologists. Sadly, many Christians worship at its altar.

In my years of experience as a Bible-believing pastor, I have observed that as people in my churches have gone to psychologists or therapists, they have come back even more confused and troubled than before they went. Some of the most blatant and unscriptural counsel I have ever heard has come from counselors in the area of marriage counseling. (Even more tragically, some of these counselors have advertised themselves as Christians.)

I have had the unhappy task of counseling people after they have been to their marriage counselor or therapist. People have come back and told me how the therapist or psychologist counseled them just to go ahead and get a divorce. Believe it or not, some have counseled them to have affairs to try out other people. Some counseled, "Just file for a divorce to get his/her attention." Not only is such advice unscriptural, it often is plain stupid!

You will soon discern this author has little sympathy for behavioral psychology or secular marriage counselors. Here is why:

Modern secular psychology has for its foundation practical atheism. The average psychologists or therapists may not "counsel" their clients there is no God; they just ignore Him. Philosophically, the modern psychology movement has these premises: (1) there is no God; (2) the Bible is bunk; and (3) "scientific research" in human behavior holds the answers to social, behavioral and emotional problems. In their view, this certainly includes marriage difficulties.

A FALSE FOUNDATION

The very foundation of modern psychology is critically flawed. It routinely holds a flawed concept of the human persona. That foundational flaw is the view of mankind. Conventional wisdom holds that man is comprised of two basic constituent

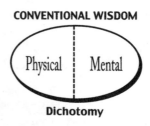

CONVENTIONAL WISDOM

Physical | Mental

Dichotomy

parts. That wisdom teaches we have a physical body which is physiological (or biological). We also have a brain which is mental (and emotional). In short, secular science begins with the conventional wisdom that states man is a *dichotomy*. He has a body which is physical and a mind which is mental. If there are problems in our physical body, we go to a medical doctor. However, if there is a nonmedical problem in our lives, we should go to a psychologist or psychiatrist. Therefore, for asocial behavior, emotional instability, troubles with pediatric behavior, marriage problems, personality defects, etc., conventional wisdom (encouraged by the "helping professions") teaches we should go to a psychologist, social worker or perhaps a psychiatrist.

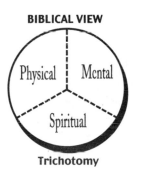

BIBLICAL VIEW

Trichotomy

The truth is, man is a *trichotomy*, not a dichotomy! The Bible clearly teaches each individual of the human race has three constituent parts: a body which is physical, a mind which is mental, and a spirit which is spiritual. The Scripture says our spirit is the pilot of our lives on an individual level. Our spirit, or our heart, as it often is referred to in the Bible, controls and directs our lives.

My spirit (or my heart) directs and influences my mind. My mind (including its emotions) in turn influences my physical body. My human spirit is like the relationship between an automobile and its driver. A modern automobile has an efficient and powerful engine. It has all of the associated hardware, such as transmission, steering, braking, suspension and electrical systems, as well as a body to provide conveyance for the passengers. It has both electrical and mechanical control systems so that the engine, steering, braking, lighting and signaling systems may be controlled. Until a driver takes control of the vehicle and properly uses the controls, the automobile won't go anywhere. It is the driver who steers and controls the car.

Likewise, on the human level, it is our spirit which directs, influences and steers our lives. The spirit is at the very heart of the human being. I am not referring to the cardiac organ that pumps blood within our chest cavity from the time of our birth until the time of our death. I refer to the spiritual heart of our being which the Bible refers to as our human spirit. It is the pilot of our lives. It is the driver of our being. It is the center of our person. It is more important than any physiological organ or system in our body. It is more important than our various mental apparatuses and functions, such as the nervous system, memory, cognitive processes or emotions. In the overall scope of individual lives, it is our human spirit which is the controlling force of life.

The problem with modern psychology and social therapy is, they either ignore or categorically reject the idea of a human spirit. As we shall soon see, the Bible makes it clear our person is comprised of not only a body and a mind but also of a spirit.

As I write this chapter, the major news of the day is about an airline crash in another state wherein scores of people have lost their lives. Indeed, it is a great tragedy. On the news networks, the commentators have pointed out how not long ago this particular airline had another crash. It was caused by pilot error.

The human tragedies which take place from day to day in people's lives and marriages in most cases are because of "pilot error." That pilot is their human spirit.

Because an academic discipline (namely, psychology) ignores or through prejudicial bias rejects one-third of the essence of the human persona, I question its judgment altogether. Furthermore, what's more crucial is that psychology and sociology have missed the most important aspect of our being, namely our spirit. How can one have confidence in a so-called science that is so foundationally incorrect in its understanding of the constituent parts of our being?

A FALSE HOPE

Poor, miserable individuals have been programmed to believe if there is trouble in their lives apart from medical problems, they should immediately see a psychologist, psychiatrist or some sort of therapist. Their counsel and advice is usually off-base because their understanding of the human persona is truncated. These "professionals," in part, are victims of their education and professional training. They usually willingly reject or ignore anything which suggests a spiritual dimension of mankind. This is particularly true when a spiritual nature relates to the Bible or Bible-based Christianity.

Years ago a teenage girl came to me and related a sordid story of how she had been forced into virtual prostitution by her own father. She said that when his friends came over, she was forced to service their base desires. She was desperate and did not know where to turn.

She sat across from me in my office and told me she was planning to kill herself. I asked her how she planned to do it.

"With a gun."

"Where's the gun?"

"Right here." Having said that, she straightened out her arm. As her hand emerged from the sleeve of her winter jacket, a pistol also emerged, pointed straight at me. As the gun slid down the length of her jacket arm, the hammer of the revolver snagged on the fabric and cocked itself. After a tense moment I asked her to give me the gun, and she did.

Because of the horrible condition of her home situation and because she was suicidal, she checked herself into a state mental hospital. In the following weeks, I visited her periodically. I asked her about the treatment, counseling and therapy she was receiving. None of it seemed of any great value to me. From week to week it seemed almost contradictory. Therefore, I asked an old friend, who had graduated from a big university with a degree in psychology, why the state psychologists were following the course they were. His reply has stuck with me though that incident was years ago. He said, "They really aren't sure what they are doing."

After several months of contradictory psychobabble, called therapy, the state institution released this troubled teenage girl. Not much changed in her life; especially was there little alleviation of her inner turmoil. That poor girl has gone on with life.

The longer I am in the ministry, the less and less confidence I have in behavioral psychology. It begins with a flawed understanding of the foundation and essence of human nature—the false premise that mankind is a dichotomy comprised of body and mind. The Bible, however, teaches mankind is a trichotomy comprised of a body, mind and a spirit. In matters concerning behavior and human relationships, the crucial factor is our spirit.

WHAT SAITH THE SCRIPTURES?

I believe the Bible is the written Word of God. It directly claims to be inspired of God. In II Timothy 3:16 the Apostle Paul wrote, "All scripture is given by inspiration of God, and is profitable…for instruction in righteousness."

I will be very forthright in crediting those precepts for our own pleasant and enduring marriage. We have had a marriage which has been heaven on earth because we have from the outset sought to build it upon the principles set forth in the Bible. The conviction that you or I am a trichotomy is based on the Bible. This is important in establishing an understanding of human nature and the subsequent issues of life. It also is important in determining where to turn for marital counsel.

As already mentioned, modern psychology and sociology begin with the philosophical foundation that humanity is essentially a composite of the physical and the mental. Moreover, it is presumed that even the mental and emotional portions of our being are ultimately biological. Because the brain is a physical organ of the body, it also can be treated and altered with various drugs and chemicals, euphemistically known as *medicine*. Therefore, modern psychiatry and psychology frequently address behavioral and emotional problems (disorders) as things to be treated by various drugs or chemicals. Hence, when family problems or personal troubles occur, our culture has conditioned people to run to the friendly neighborhood psychologist or therapist.

The realization that we have a spirit in addition to our mind is a concept anchored in Scripture. This understanding is crucial in developing a happy, solid marriage. It is even more crucial in trying to reconcile a strained marital union.

I THESSALONIANS 5:23

The Apostle Paul, in writing to the church at Thessalonica, said, "And the very God of peace sanctify you wholly; and I pray God your whole spirit and soul and body be preserved blameless unto the coming of our Lord Jesus Christ." Notice how the apostle in one immediate context mentioned three constituent parts of the human

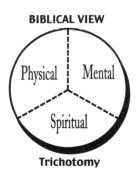

BIBLICAL VIEW

Physical | Mental

Spiritual

Trichotomy

existence. He referred to the **spirit** and the **soul** and the **body**.

There is insight in the Greek words from which these are translated. The word translated "spirit" comes from the Greek word *pneuma* from which our English word *pneumatic* is derived. It is the common word used in referring to our spirit. The word translated "body" comes from the Greek word *soma* and again is the common word used to refer to our human bodies.

What is of particular interest is the word from which "soul" is translated. This is the word *psyche* in Greek. It sounds familiar, doesn't it? It is the basic root from which stem all our English derivatives, such as *psychology, psychiatrist, psychoanalyze,* etc.

As we will soon see, it is our *spirit* which will have a crucial bearing upon a fulfilled marriage relationship. The weakness of modern psychology is that it ignores this crucial aspect of the human persona.

HEBREWS 4:12

The scriptural penman of Hebrews 4:12 wrote, "For the word of God is quick, and powerful, and sharper than any twoedged sword, piercing even to the dividing asunder of soul and spirit, and of the joints and marrow, and is a discerner of the thoughts and intents of the heart." Notice that the Scripture distinguishes between our soul and our spirit. It uses the analogy of how marrow is in distinction to the joint or the bone. Our spirit, though integrally related to our mind, nevertheless is distinct, even as marrow is integrally related to the bone and is yet distinct. Marrow is unseen, yet it is at the very center of the bone and is crucial to life. Likewise, our human spirit is unseen, but it is vital to the total person.

Here the Holy Spirit also refers to another interesting

word. That is the word *heart*. In the context of this verse, the Scripture refers to how the Word of God is able to discern between the thoughts and intents of the heart. The Greek word at this point is *kardia*, from which our common English word *cardiac* is derived. However, it is evident from the context that this passage is not referring to the cardiac organ pumping blood through our body. Rather, it is a clear reference to the spiritual heart of our being.

Thayer's Greek Lexicon (which is a standard Greek dictionary) defines *kardia* (apart from its physical **HUMAN SPIRIT** = **SPIRITUAL HEART** reference to the circulatory system) as "the seat and center of the spirit." Hence, we discover our spirit and our spiritual heart have a close relationship. Our heart evidently is where our spirit resides. On a practical level, the concepts of the human spirit and spiritual heart are used synonymously and interchangeably throughout the Bible. Therefore, for all practical purposes, we might equate the concept of our human spirit with our spiritual heart.

THE SOURCE OF THE PROBLEM

This leads us to a major spiritual problem: how is our human spirit (or heart) naturally depraved and distorted? As we approach our discussion of the ingredients of a heavenly marriage, this understanding is of paramount importance.

In Jeremiah 17:9, the Bible says, "The **heart** is deceitful above all things, and desperately wicked: who can know it?" The unvarnished truth is, our human heart (or spirit) is naturally deceitful and desperately wicked. The spiritual pilot that guides my life is naturally wicked! My human spirit (or heart) on a natural level is intrinsically evil.

As we proceed, it will be evident certain things are damaging to marriage relationships. For example, in many a home there are constant verbal sniping and nastiness of the tongue. Jesus said:

"But those things which proceed out of the mouth come forth from the heart; and they defile the man. For out of the heart proceed evil thoughts, murders, adulteries, fornications, thefts, false witness, blasphemies."—Matt. 15:18,19.

The problem of a nasty tongue is actually a heart problem. Obviously, adultery is a critical and sometimes fatal wound to a marriage. Jesus Christ said the problem of adultery comes from the human heart. Therefore, it is ultimately a spiritual problem.

The problem is on the inside and therefore is fundamentally spiritual. Most problems which crop up in our lives and marriages have their origins in our hearts. The psychologist cannot treat these because he doesn't believe we 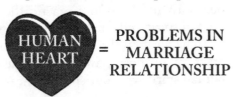 each have a spirit or spiritual heart. The therapist never gets to the root of the trouble because he is oblivious to the existence of the human spirit.

"GOD saw that the wickedness of man was great in the earth, and that every imagination of the thoughts of his heart was only evil continually" (Gen. 6:5). The evening news telecasts and the newspapers reiterate the fact that we live in a time of great wickedness, and the Bible says that the source of this wickedness is the human heart. Problems in the national culture or in our marriage relationships stem from the human heart.

We have a human spirit which is naturally and intrinsically evil. When two people live together in a unit as close and intimate as a marriage relationship, it is crucial their hearts be in harmony and their evil impulses restrained.

The foundational premise of this book is, *The issues of life are fundamentally spiritual.* The advice and principles contained herein are derived from the establishment of this fact.

HEAVENLY MARRIAGE

SPIRITUAL PRINCIPLES

If we would have marriages which are heaven on earth, we must build our lives on a solid spiritual foundation, and we must deal with our naturally sinful human hearts.

The primary source Book and pole of authority from which we will speak is the Bible. It, by its very nature, has the answers for the human heart. "For the word of God is...a discerner of the thoughts and intents of the **heart**" (Heb. 4:12). The keys to the problems of human nature and behavior are found in the Bible. Its Author is the Holy Spirit, and its message is directed toward our spirits. The God who designed and created us has written the Book of instructions and explanations for our journey through life. That Book is the Bible.

3.

THE ISSUES OF LIFE ARE FUNDAMENTALLY SPIRITUAL

THE ISSUES OF LIFE

As we continue to lay a foundation for the main thrust of this book—a marriage that is heaven on earth—let us delve more deeply into one of its basic premises: that is, **the issues of life are fundamentally spiritual.**

Proverbs 4:23 says, "Keep thy heart with all diligence; for out of it are the issues of life." The issues of life—the important things of life; the intangible things of life; the matters that relate to happiness, family and fulfillment—are fundamentally spiritual; that is, the issues of life are rooted in the human spirit and are fulfilled through spiritual principles outlined in the Word of God.

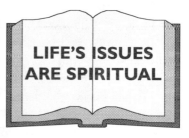

As mentioned in the preceding chapter, the world around us largely ignores the spiritual dimension of human existence. With the prevailing secular culture of scientific investigation, if something cannot be placed into a test tube and empirically or analytically studied, it is largely ignored. However, the fact that spiritual things are in a dimension which cannot be physically analyzed offers no rationale to ignore them. Yet the secular "scientific" mentality of the age in fact routinely ignores the spiritual aspect of life. The chaos the world is in illustrates this fallacy. Our society demonstrates the truth of the Apostle Paul's words written nineteen hundred years ago, "Professing themselves to be wise, they became fools" (Rom. 1:22).

Let us look at several broad areas of life illustrating this principle. More than one hundred years ago, Karl Marx wrote his treatise *Das Kapital,* which became the bible for the communist world in the next century. **Marx's premise was, the issues of life are fundamentally** *economic.* **Therefore,** according to him, all economic activity must be controlled and centralized by the state to provide equality and fairness. In his opinion, all people should be equal economically. A major doctrine of his communist

LIFE'S ISSUES

ARE ECONOMIC

scheme, "from each according to his ability, to each according to his need," was based upon the assumption that man is fundamentally decent and good. All that was needed was for the proletariat (workers) to throw off the shackles and chains of the oppressive bourgeois capitalists. Then, through the process of state-sponsored socialism, pure communism would emerge, which would be the workers' paradise.

We all know it did not turn out that way. Though the communists delivered state-sponsored socialism at the tip of a bayonet, there never was any pure communism, much less a workers' paradise. The fatal flaw in not only their forced socialism but also their hoped-for communism was a fundamental misunderstanding of human nature. Communists and their liberal counterparts in the West have routinely assumed that man is intrinsically decent and good. If his negative environment or oppressive chains can be eradicated, the utopia will emerge. Moreover, they, like the mental health community of the world today, ignored and rejected the premise that man has a spirit which controls his life.

The fact is, the human heart is deceitful and desperately wicked. Communism, and even socialism, will not work because of the essence of human nature. Not only did the communists suppress the natural freedom for enterprise intrinsic in the human heart; they critically misunderstood the flawed, sinful, *spiritual* nature of the human heart. Communism was based on a faulty foundation. Even the economic issues in life have their roots in spiritual principles.

Likewise, our own government over the past several generations has held that **the issues of life are fundamentally** *governmental.* Hence, whenever there is a problem perceived in our society, the government proposes and usually passes some new government program.

LIFE'S ISSUES

ARE GOVERNMENTAL

Therefore, when education scores are down and school problems are up, the conventional wisdom in Washington and state legislatures is to spend more government money on some new government program designed to fix the problem; but the problems in education more often than not are spiritual. Children who are undisciplined in their spirits and teachers who have been trained in a "let-them-do-their-own-thing" philosophy together produce one big mess with little real education resulting.

One major key to education is discipline. This involves discipline of the mind to learn, discipline within the classroom, and discipline to do what ought to be done. These are essentially spiritual principles. Yet this idea is largely ignored in American education today.

As mentioned in the preceding chapter, psychology and the "social sciences" routinely ignore the human spirit.

Accordingly, they frequently prescribe various drugs and chemicals to try to "treat" antisocial behavior which is at its root spiritual in nature. Guilt, selfishness, lust, anger, hatred, fear, deviousness, and such like, are spiritual problems that can be dealt with only by a spiritual solution.

As we approach the ingredients which make a happy marriage, it is noteworthy that the positive qualities of life which we all seek are spiritual. When our hearts are clouded by anger, hurt feelings, worry, hatred, bitterness and selfishness, for example, we will not be happy. All these problems are spiritual by their very nature, and they are common to marriage.

SPIRITUAL PRINCIPLES

✞ Peace With God

The Bible contains a number of basic principles necessary to produce peace of heart, and all of them are spiritual in nature. Before we can ever have the peace *of* God, we must first be at peace *with* God (Rom. 5:1). That is a spiritual transaction through faith in Jesus Christ.

✞ Peace of God

Then the Bible teaches such spiritual attributes as righteousness, trust in the Lord, obedience to God, along with a love for God's Word, as prerequisites for peace of heart. Only when we have the peace of God in our hearts will we be truly happy. The issues of life are indeed fundamentally spiritual.

✞ Discipline of Life

Again, our human existence is a trichotomy of body, mind *and spirit*. It is the control by our spirit of our mind and ultimately of our body that results in a disciplined life. Because people are not naturally disciplined, they tolerate all kinds of weaknesses and shortcomings. Such undesirable conditions may be as common as being overweight or as intangible as procrastination instead of punctuality. Discipline of life is essentially spiritual in nature. Again, the issues of life are fundamentally spiritual.

✟ Righteousness

A basic spiritual quality which undergirds all facets of our lives is righteousness. Righteousness is simply doing what is right. It is doing right as a matter of principle that governs the ethical and moral structure of our lives. Such sought-for qualities as integrity and honesty may be attained simply by doing what is right. Righteousness by its very nature is spiritual. We must let it dominate every area of our lives.

✟ Sexual Morality

Sexual morality is predicated upon the principle of doing right morally (or sexually). The sin-sick world in which we live is willingly ignorant of the fact that sexual immorality (fornication and adultery) is at the very root of many of its troubles. God has ordained one place for human physical intimacy. That is within the parameters of the marriage relationship. Yet people in the world routinely live in sexual unrighteousness, be it premarital sexual activity (fornication), extramarital sexual activity (adultery) or homosexuality. The result is universal misery.

THE PROBLEMS ARE SPIRITUAL

I have watched this miserable cycle repeatedly.

Some guy, to satisfy the lusts of his flesh, pressures his girlfriend until she finally gives in, and they begin living in sin. She is a little nervous about it. Sooner or later the inevitable happens: she winds up pregnant. He is not interested in getting married and soon leaves her. She is left to carry the child *alone*, in every sense of the word.

In the ensuing weeks and months, she must contend with a diverse spectrum of emotions. She has a sense of guilt for yielding her virginity to such a "skunk." Therefore, she becomes angry at him. There are days of depression and anxiety over the future. Yet she thought she loved him.

The day of delivering her child arrives, and she becomes a mother. Now she has to contend with supporting herself and her child. Consequently, she becomes involved in the social welfare system. Her rapport with her parents has deteriorated; therefore, she and her child live on the edge of poverty. She lives in a dowdy apartment in a rundown section of town. She has to contend with finding transportation for such common chores as going to the grocery store. She bears one hundred percent of the burden of actually rearing her child. The guy who got her pregnant is sporadic in paying child support. On top of it all, she has the lingering effects of a sexually transmitted disease she received from him.

Meanwhile, she catches the attention of another fellow at a local night spot. As he shows her interest and kindness, they inevitably wind up in bed together at her apartment. The guy moves in with her and helps pay the bills, but before long the inevitable signs of pregnancy are present. He gets nervous and is no longer on the scene. The welfare system pays for the delivery of her second child, and the whole sad cycle begins all over.

She is in a trap. She has difficulty finding a job which will make it worth her effort to pay a day-care provider. There is the cost of transportation to work. She has barely enough money to survive on. With her children, it is difficult to further her education. So she continues living on welfare in a rundown apartment in a bad neighborhood, with two crying children. The only male attention she can attract is from the same kind of lowlifes who got her pregnant previously.

This sad scenario is true of multitudes all over our country every year. It is the focus of politicians and government programs. We hear much about poverty, single parents, latchkey children, crime and welfare costs. Here is the thing that the evening news won't tell you: **the root of this whole mess is** *spiritual*.

This stereotypical young woman and the young men knew it was *not right* **to have premarital sex. They didn't need more sex education. They knew what was right and what was wrong and the consequences of doing wrong. However, they** *chose* **the wrong anyway.**

Jesus said, "For out of the **heart** proceed...fornications." The girl's choice to "do it" with her boyfriend was ultimately a spiritual choice. She knew she *ought not* to do it, but she did it anyway.

All the rationalizations—like "Well, everybody is doing it"; or, "Well, it's the nineties, and I'll choose to do with my body as I please"; or, "Well, maybe if I get pregnant, he will marry me"—are hollow. She knew right, and in her heart she chose to do wrong. That is a spiritual matter.

Don't you see how the poverty and social problems, not to mention the heartache and personal entrapment, have been brought upon her because of spiritual decisions? Whether it was right, wise or moral was not important to her. She knew it was not right, wise nor moral, but she did it anyway. She made crucial, life-changing decisions because she *wanted* to do what she did.

America is in the mess it is in today because of similar moral and spiritual decisions that are made thousands of times each day across the land. **The issues of life are fundamentally spiritual!**

Consider this scenario: Our above-described young lady finally does get married. She tries to straighten up and "fly right." However, the guy she finally married is not much different from her two previous "live-ins." She met him at a nightclub. She was dressed provocatively, and that very night they wound up sleeping together. When she got pregnant again, he agreed to marry her.

Between her AFDC checks and his income, they managed to get ahead a little. They moved into a better neighborhood. By then the children were going to school, and she could find work. They became a two-income family. On Friday nights, though, he liked to get drunk at the local bar. She really was not sure if she could trust him. She knew she had picked him up in a bar, and she knew that there were other girls there who wouldn't mind doing the same thing.

She stayed home with the children. When he came home drunk, they fought. He came to consider her a nag and referred to her as "the old lady" among his friends. In his heart he knew it wasn't right to get drunk and flirt with the girls at the bar, but he chose to do it anyway. She knew it was not right to call him all kinds of nasty names, but she did it anyway, getting some meager satisfaction in that form of limited retaliation.

Both of them had made decisions based upon what they *wanted* to do and ignoring their consciences that told them what was wrong. That is *spiritual*. The Bible says drunkenness is a work of the old spiritual nature which is called our flesh (Gal. 5:17–21). The girl knows she ought not be so mean with her tongue, but in her heart she chooses to do it anyway. That is *spiritual*.

He likes to fish and hunt. Because things are less than utopia at home, he begins to spend more and more time out fishing. He enjoys getting out with the guys, hoisting a few beers, and playing with the dog. At least the dog wags its tail—and not its tongue—when he comes home from work.

He becomes more selfish with his discretionary income.

He buys a boat for fishing. His wife, as expected, gives him grief about that. They bicker about how he spends his money. He really doesn't care what his "old lady" thinks. He enjoys his time out with the guys. So what that he's spending more and more money on the boat? He has always wanted a bigger motor. Besides, if he is going to catch any fish, he needs all those fancy electronics and that fishing gear. So what if he comes home a little crocked? If he can drive safely, what's it to her? "It's my life, and I'll live it as I please!" he says.

Well, by now she is getting really fed up with his selfish and ugly moods. She is tired of taking care of the house and the kids while he is out enjoying himself. One day at work she notices one of the guys there has his eye on her. She flirts with him a little. He seems like such a nice guy—kind, considerate and levelheaded. He seems to have his head on straight. They begin to eat their lunches together at break time. She fixes herself up a bit more for work and starts wearing clothing that is a little more revealing.

One day he suggests they go out for coffee after work. She knows that she really shouldn't, but her husband is such a selfish, immature jerk. "Well, why not?" After several such little meetings, they find themselves in a motel room. She knows it is not *right*, "but what's the big diff'? He's a lot better than what's at home." She willfully chooses to commit adultery.

Did not Jesus say, "Out of the heart proceed...adulteries"? The decision she has made is *spiritual*. She knew it was wrong, but she did it anyway. **The issues of life are indeed fundamentally spiritual!**

In due season the husband will find out what is

ALL DECISIONS **=** **SPIRITUAL DECISIONS**
ALL CHOICES **=** **SPIRITUAL CHOICES**

going on. There will be some terrible fights. Tension will set in over that family like a cold war. There will be the visit to the attorney's office. Divorce proceedings will be underway. A marriage that had turned into a hell on earth will dissolve.

* * *

Let us shift to a different social league. As I develop this stereotypical, composite story, I will add fictitious names to the characters. Though this story is not of any certain real people, the pieces of the mosaic have come from true-to-life situations.

Dick had met Carol in college. After graduation they married. While he held a position in the government, she went on and finished her master's degree. Then she too went to work using her training to start a career. They enjoyed socializing. The highlight for Carol's week was to get together with friends on a Saturday night and have a little party.

As they progressed professionally, they built a new house in a nice suburban subdivision. It had all the nice little things "yuppies" like to have—a Jacuzzi, a cedar deck with a gas grill and a double-car garage. Carol decorated the living room and formal dining room tastefully and spared no expense. Their two-car garage had two late-model vehicles parked in it. Monday morning Dick would head off to work in his conservative business suit, and Carol would head off to her office as well. Things seemed to be going great. The neighbors figured Dick and Carol "had it made."

Little by little, however, a cold war was developing within that nice suburban home. When the baby came, Carol took a leave of absence from her job to take care of the baby. They figured that they could make it on Dick's income. Unfortunately, Carol still liked to spend money as she was accustomed to doing, but she figured there was no need for worry: her pocketbook had several trusty credit cards. She used them. She knew that she really shouldn't do that, but she *chose* to do it anyway. Though her better judgment told her it was not wise, she *wanted* to charge things; therefore, she went ahead and did so.

When the bills arrived each month, invariably an argument broke out between her and Dick. He wanted to know why she had spent so much. She scornfully reminded him that she was a part of this family too! Their fighting would be hot and vociferous for a time, but then it would settle into an icebox where neither spoke to the other for days.

As time progressed, Carol became the *de facto* leader of the house. She would fly into a rage or into tears to get her way. She nagged and badgered, and Dick just let her "rule the roost," trying to keep some peace in the home. She knew her nasty tongue was not right. But so what? She was just saying how she *felt!*

She liked sweets. As calories and age increased, she put on obvious weight. Because of her weight, she cajoled Dick into doing much of the housework. Though he held a full-time position and she was home most of the time, it was he who scrubbed the floors and cleaned the toilets. He vacuumed the house on Saturday and took care of the laundry. Yet Carol complained that she didn't have enough time for her bowling league, PTA stuff and the ladies' guild at church. She joined a weight-reduction club and worked out some but never lost much weight. She knew every little craft shop in town and was a regular customer at the mall.

She could be so sweet and cooperative; but if things didn't go her way, she became highly irritable. She wanted new living room furniture. Dick complained they couldn't afford it, whereupon she skillfully went into one of her combination acts of tears, pouting, giving him the cold shoulder and sarcasm. It seemed to Dick that when he came home from work each day, he was always walking into a buzz saw.

Carol decided she wanted to redecorate the master bathroom and bedroom. Again Dick protested, but she went ahead and did it anyway.

Physical intimacy for them became almost nonexistent. Dick, for the most part, just was not in the mood for romance when bedtime came. He harbored resentment and anger toward his wife. Because she had gained weight, she wasn't exactly "Miss America" anymore. Consequently, that aspect of their marriage dwindled to near extinction.

Well, one day a new secretary by the name of Sheila was hired at Dick's office. She had a pleasant personality and was efficient, and Dick could not help but notice her physical attractiveness. As time marched on, he would confide in his secretary as to how things at home were not exactly super-duper. She felt sorry for him. He was such a nice guy. She knew from Carol's calls to the office that she could be a shrew.

Dick sensed his secretary was sympathetic to his unhappiness. They would sit and talk during the lunch hour. She became the one to whom he could pour out his troubles.

One evening Sheila's car was broken down, and Dick offered to take her home. When they pulled up to her apartment building, they paused to talk a little. Dick felt his hand resting on her knee. As they prepared to part, Sheila leaned over and placed a kiss on Dick's cheek. His heart fluttered.

One thing led to another, and Dick and Sheila began having an affair. Eventually Carol found out about it, and the volcano erupted. "How could you ever do this to me?" she screamed. The cold war had escalated into a hot war. Their marriage had deteriorated into hell on earth.

Let's analyze a few things in this home. Carol knew she shouldn't be so bossy and selfish. She knew it wasn't *right*, but she did it anyway. That was a spiritual decision. She knew she shouldn't indulge in overeating, but she would rather do what she *wanted* than do what she *ought*. That again was a spiritual decision. She knew it *wasn't right* to be so sharp with her tongue. Again, that was the way she *felt*, so she "let it rip." That was a spiritual decision.

Dick knew things were progressing to the point of no return with Sheila. He knew it wasn't *right;* nevertheless, he followed his *desires*. He knew adultery was *not right,* but he did it anyway. **All these decisions are spiritual in nature.**

Jesus Christ said, "Out of the abundance of the heart the mouth speaketh" (Matt. 12:34); "For from within, out of the heart of men, proceed evil thoughts, adulteries...covetousness...pride, foolishness" (Mark 7:21,22). The issues of life remain fundamentally spiritual. Spiritual decisions have consequences that affect every area of our lives.

∗   ∗   ∗

Let us view another composite of stories. When George and Anne had been dating, they had drunk together, done drugs together, slept together and agreed together to have an abortion when she got pregnant. Ironically, both had been brought up in a Bible-believing church and knew right from wrong.

Eventually they got married. George loved his rock music, his cigarettes, his beer and doing drugs from time to time. Anne went right along with her husband and did all he did. She was guilty of self-indulgent living as much as he, but in her heart she knew it was not right. She told George, "We need to get back to church and get right with the Lord."

He said, "Yeah, one of these days."

As time progressed, the drinking got heavier, and the drug usage, more frequent. They began to fight. Though they were basically on the same wavelength spiritually— backslidden and far from God—they surely didn't get along with each other anymore. She wanted to "do her thing," and he wanted to do his. They fought all of the time. You name it—they fought about it.

As the situation deteriorated, he became verbally abusive. He called her every vulgar and low-down name he could think of. Finally she went home to her parents, and he just kept on "doing his thing." The marriage never recovered. They split and went their separate ways.

Spiritual practices were at work in this instance also. Their relationship from the beginning had been based upon satisfying their physical desires. The concept of sacrificial love was something that neither seemed to comprehend. They both lived for themselves and were miserable because of the wear of it. All this had profound spiritual implications. Self-centered living is antithetical to genuine spiritual love. The issues of their lives were fouled by the lack of spiritual principles.

> **ALL FAULTS**
> **=**
> **SPIRITUAL FAULTS**

* * *

I feel sure the following story is typical in a significant percentage of marriages.

Jim and Jan had been married for years. There was no alcohol involved in the marriage. There was no infidelity. There was no physical abuse or physical fighting. They lived in a comfortable home. Their children were for the most part decent kids. They both were active in their church. He had a respectable position in the community. She likewise was active in community affairs and activities. The neighbors thought they were nice people.

Inside the privacy of their house, however, there was a strained relationship. At one time or another, each of them had thought of getting a divorce. Maybe they stayed together because of the kids. Maybe it was due to the fact they were relatively better off financially by keeping the marriage together. In any event, their marriage was being held together by the flimsiest of threads.

Jim was stubborn and self-centered. His hobbies and interests were what was important to him. He liked to fish. He liked to hunt. He liked to bowl. He liked to putter in his shop out in the garage. He liked to watch his football and basketball in the winter. He liked to golf. He liked to go to local athletic events and cheer. He liked to take part in union activities and was part of a local community service organization. Jim liked to do what he liked to do.

When Jan would complain about his self-centered living, he became a bear. "Hey, I'm a big boy. I bring home a good paycheck. I pay the bills. I fix the house. My life is *my* life! I'll do my own thing! Now buzz off!" For the rest of the week, there would be an icy strain between them. The children knew it, but they steered clear. They knew better than to interfere.

As time passed on, Jan became cynical and bitter. She confided in her mother that she had made a big mistake when she married Jim. Jan was no "Polly Purebred" herself. She knew how to be catty. She could lay on sarcasm like butter on a knife. Though she at times held her tongue, at other times she heaped scorn and all manner of nastiness on her husband.

The sad thing about it is, both knew better. Both were born-again Christians. Both attended a Bible-believing church. Both knew it was wrong to have such a bitter and sour personal relationship. However, pride and stubbornness kept both of them from yielding. Neither of them had it in him or her ever to make more than a token gesture of asking forgiveness. Apologies were perfunctory and cold.

The problem in marriages such as Jan and Jim's is patently spiritual. One party lived in self-centeredness. Both were stubborn and proud. Both could use their tongues as weapons. Each harbored bitterness and animosity toward the other. All these are spiritual problems! The issues of life are fundamentally spiritual.

*   *   *

The issues of life are fundamentally spiritual. Each of these stories has been a composite of problems that are typical in so many American families, and underlying each story are spiritual problems.

In the following chapters we will outline step-by-step the building of a marriage that has a genuinely spiritual foundation. We will go to the Word of God and detail God's plan for a marriage that is heaven on earth.

SECTION II

BUILDING BLOCKS OF A HEAVENLY MARRIAGE

As we progress from problems typical in so many marriages, let us begin to identify from the Scripture the building blocks necessary for a wonderful marriage. For a home to be heaven on earth there needs to be a proper foundation. In that foundation will be spiritual building blocks. We will consider several foundational principles and look at each in some detail.

4.

AGAPE LOVE

WHAT IS *AGAPE* LOVE?

English is a hybrid language with contributions or influences from the Latin, Greek, French, Anglo-Saxon, Norse, Welsh, Celtic and other languages. Each of these languages has colored our spoken tongue in an interesting way.

The New Testament was written in Greek. A considerable portion of our English language has connections to Greek. Therefore, as we refer to the Bible—and the New Testament in particular—we will allude to the concepts underpinning words in the Greek language.

The Greek language of New Testament times used several words which today are commonly translated *love*. Those three words are *agape* (pronounced "ah-*gay*-pay"), *phileo* (pronounced "fil-*ay*-oh"), and *eros* (pronounced "*air*-os"). In this chapter, we will focus on *agape* love. The following chapter will develop the concepts of *phileo*. *Eros,* referring to sexual love, does not appear in the New Testament, and we will not consider it in this book.

Agape love is the highest form of love. It is the concept used overwhelmingly in the New Testament. For example, in John 3:16, "For God so *loved* the world," the word used is *agape*. In Galatians 2:20, Christ "*loved* me, and gave himself for me," the word is *agape*. In I John 4:8, "God is *love*," the word is *agape*. In Ephesians 5:25, "Husbands, *love* your wives," the word is *agape*.

Though the word is routinely translated "love" (sometimes "charity"), the distinctive essence of the thought of it is "a giving of one's self for another." It is the essence of selflessness. It is, by its very nature, others-oriented. There is little or no reflection of oneself in *agape* love.

Therefore, when "God so loved the world...**he gave** his only begotten Son." God loved us to such an extent that *He gave*. But not only did He give, He gave what was the dearest to Him—Jesus Christ, His Son. *Agape* love is giving from the very heart.

Galatians 2:20 says that Christ not only loved us, He *gave* Himself for us. "Christ also hath loved us, and hath given himself for us" (Eph. 5:2). The love of Jesus Christ toward us is amplified by the thought that He has given Himself for us. The word again is *agape*.

Ephesians 5:25 is an interesting verse for our purposes because here the love of Christ is likened to the love husbands ought to have for their wives. There we read, "Husbands, *love* your wives, even as Christ also *loved* the church, and gave himself for it." Both times the word used is *agape*. Notice again how such love is described by the example of a giving of self.

The highest form of love is *agape* love. After twenty-five years of observing and working with families, I am convinced **a major problem in many marriages is a lack of real love.**

Let us develop the idea further. Jesus said, "Thou shalt love the Lord thy God with all thy **heart,** and...thy neighbour as thyself" (Matt. 22:37,39). Though Jesus here mentioned the other constituent parts of our being as well, it seems clear that *agape* love ultimately emanates from the heart. That makes it spiritual. (We earlier established the definition of the *heart* as "the seat and center of the spirit.") *Agape* love comes from the heart. It emanates from the spirit. It is spiritual. I belabor this because we are going to see that the other types of love relate more to the other portions of our being.

"See that ye love one another with a pure **heart** fervently" (I Pet. 1:22). Again, the word used for *love* is *agape*. Notice that *agape* love emanates from the heart. Selfless, giving love is spiritual.

I have noticed that the average person doesn't really understand much about what genuine love is. I have asked numerous people—in counseling situations, teaching situations and other forums—the definition of *love*. Usually I drew only blank stares. We talk about love all the time, but most people can't define it.

A popular song some years ago said, "What the world needs now is love, sweet love." Yet of all the segments of our culture, it seems that popular music has the most distorted idea of love. In the world's music, love is usually set forth in the context of wanting. So the stereotypical popular singer croons, "I want you; I need you; I gotta have you; I can't live without you" in the context of "love." The focus of the message in such music is of getting, or the desire to have someone. The focal point is *me*—what *I* want, what *I* need, what *I* desire. That is *getting*, not *giving*.

There is an aspect of love that relates to physical intimacy; however, so much of what the world speaks about in terms of "love" could more accurately be labeled "lust." Lust is seeking to satisfy our own desires. It is seeking to gratify our own urges. It is accomplishing the conquest of another person. The world speaks and sings about such in the context of "love" when it is actually lust. It is getting instead of giving. It emanates from the body and not the spirit.

Many a young woman has sacrificed her purity to the age-old line, "If you loved me, you would let me do it." That comes not from love but of lust. The lowlife who uses such a line (and his number is legion) usually cares far less for his girlfriend than he does for his own selfish lust. He isn't interested in *giving* of himself *to* her. He is interested in *getting from* her. He isn't interested in her best interest; he is merely interested in gratifying his own lust.

Yet the world routinely talks about it as "love" or "the making of love." Ironically, the girl often does yield her body to her beau out of some degree of love for him, while the likelihood of his having any true love for her is minimal.

I CORINTHIANS 13

First Corinthians 13 is universally known as "The Love Chapter." In this classic text the Greek word *agape* is rendered "charity" in English.

"Charity suffereth long, and is kind; charity envieth not; charity vaunteth not itself, is not puffed up,

"Doth not behave itself unseemly, seeketh not her own, is not easily provoked, thinketh no evil;

"Rejoiceth not in iniquity, but rejoiceth in the truth;

"Beareth all things, believeth all things, hopeth all things, endureth all things."—I Cor. 13:4–7.

'Love suffers long' (vs. 4). The sense is of patience—in fact, of being very patient. *Love is patient*. It is willing to bear with another's shortcomings or needs. *Agape* love has its focus on the other and his/her good, his/her well-being and his/her need. By its very nature, it is neither self-directed nor self-oriented.

Moreover, *'love is kind.'* When I sit on one side of the desk in marriage counseling situations,  sometimes I am amazed at how unkind the people on the other side are to each other. Furthermore, usually the people behaving in this manner purport to love each other. Love is kind—considerate of the other, his/her feelings, his/her emotions, his/her thoughts.

When love is present, the focus is not on one's own feelings, needs or interests. It is upon the other person's. Sarcasm and kindness do not dwell in the same abode. Sharp barbs and digs do not coexist with kindness. Nastiness and vindictiveness are aliens to kindness. Love is kind.

The next time you catch yourself being foul or unkind to your mate, just remember: love is kind! Unkindness is not related to love.

Then, *'love envieth not.'* Here is another interesting word. Though I think the English word *envy* is an adequate translation, the sense in the Greek is "to boil over," as the pot of potatoes heating on the stove might do. Boiling over with envy, temper and other negative emotions is antithetical to love. It is  not on the same wavelength. It is not on the same frequency. It doesn't work together with love.

When we boil over with envy or other negative feelings toward our spouses, the origin of such negative emotion is not a heart of love. We will later identify the source of such attitudes and feelings; but here we simply state that envy and love are not related.

Moreover, *'love does not vaunt itself, nor is it puffed up.'* This deals with pride. "Nobody is going to tell *me* what to do!" "Well, who does *she* think *she* is?" "Hey, I'm a big boy; I can make my own decisions!"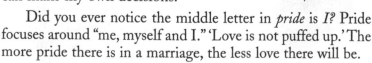

Did you ever notice the middle letter in *pride* is *I?* Pride focuses around "me, myself and I." 'Love is not puffed up.' The more pride there is in a marriage, the less love there will be.

Love *"doth not behave itself unseemly"* (I Cor. 13:5). The

word translated "unseemly" has the sense of "improperly" or "indecently." Genuine love will not take advantage of another. Love will never be the motive for moral improprieties, be they premarital or extramarital. The motive for such is self-oriented and not others-oriented. Love does not behave itself improperly.

Then, 'love does not seek her own.' In other words, *love is not selfish.* Love does not seek to get for itself. It seeks to give of itself. Love does not accumulate for self. It is giving of self.

So much of the marriage trouble I see is rooted here.

One or the other of the marriage partners lives for himself. He buys for himself. He seeks entertainment and recreation for himself. He wallows in self-pity. He wears his feelings on his sleeve. His life focuses around fulfilling himself, enjoying himself, asserting himself and getting for himself. That's the opposite of love.

'Love seeketh not her own.' (Incidentally, the personal pronoun *her* here is generic. There is no implication that it refers to the feminine gender other than in the rendering of the word from the Greek.)

Then, *'love is not easily provoked.'* The idea is of not being easily irritated. More often than not, when we become irritated, it is because our perceived interests have been crossed. Our time has been interrupted. Our desires have been put off. It all comes back to self. Love is willing to give and yield of itself.

Also, *'love does not think evil.'* When we love someone as we ought, we won't jump to conclusions about him in a negative fashion.
We will want to give him the benefit
of the doubt. We won't accept an accu-
sation or allegation against him.

LOVE DOES NOT THINK EVIL

A good illustration is the fairly
natural instinct of parents to stick up
for their children. When criticism or
problems about one's child come to light, the first reaction is
to think, *Well, my child wouldn't do that.* Whether he did or
not is beside the point. Most parents will almost instinctively not think evil about their children until compelling
evidence to the contrary is brought to bear. They love their
children and therefore don't think evil of them.

Many a marriage would be made better if one or both
spouses would be willing not to think evil of each other.
Love doesn't jump to the worse of the conclusions. It thinks
the better.

Verses 6 and 7 of the chapter essentially say that *agape*
love is not interested in wrong but in right. It puts up with
all things, it hopes for the best, and it endures whatever
comes along. One thing is certain: *agape* love is not self-
directed. Its focus is upon the need and concern of the other.
Self-love and *agape* love are not related. Moreover, *agape* love
comes from the heart and is therefore spiritual in nature.

AGAPE LOVE IS GIVING

Some stereotypical stories were given in the preceding
chapter. The basic problem in most of them was a lack of
agape love. Yet the reason so many marriages are miserable is
that one or both of the partners in each have little or no

agape love toward their spouses.

Perhaps it is the husband who lives for his big toys. In reality, he loves himself much more than he loves his wife. His focus is on *numero uno* and what pleases him. He is more interested in getting than in giving. Therefore, his focus is on his hunting, fishing and sports stuff. His interest, and not what is encouraging for his wife, is what entertains him. He is selfish. His world is like a bicycle wheel in which all the spokes are pointing inward. He is the hub, and the way he lives reflects this. The strain and pressure in his marriage are because he lives for and loves himself.

The story was given of the wife who is a battle-ax at home. She lives for her world. She is more interested in redecorating her house than in her husband. She is proud of the sharpness of her tongue, and she really is oblivious to how it is driving her husband away from her. She loves herself more than she loves her husband. She lives for her interests, pursuits, entertainments and enjoyment. In their home there is very little *agape* love.

An earlier chapter gives the stereotypical stories in which spouses were unfaithful. Though there may have been characteristics of the other mates which made infidelity more likely, when push came to shove, the unfaithful partners sinned because they *wanted* to. There was little or no consideration given to how it would devastate their spouses. The focus became fulfilling romantic infatuation and creating excitement. It was fantasy being fulfilled. It was lust and gratification being satisfied.

It all revolved around fulfilling desires. No thought was given to how this would affect the children. No thought was given to how it would wound the other spouses involved.

In fact, often in such situations little thought is given to the consequences likely to occur for the other adulterers. Each adulterer focuses upon only "me, myself and I": *my* interests, *my* desires, *my* excitement, *my* infatuation and *my* lustful gratification. There is no real love involved at any point for anyone in the situations.

The irony of it all may be that the two adulterers throw around the word *love* or the phrase *making love.* The truth of the matter is, there is no *giving of* oneself for the other. There is only a *getting for* oneself *from* the other. That is the antithesis of *agape* love.

There is no giving of self in sarcasm. There is no giving of self in impatience. There is no giving of self in unkindness. There is no giving of self in stubbornness or pride.

Agape love is a giving of one's self for the other. It comes from the heart. Therefore, it is spiritual in nature.

Agape love is active and not passive. The world has cultivated the idea that we "fall in love." Though there may be some credibility to the idea as a romance begins, "falling in love" is definitely not mature love. In the

Type of love:	*agape*
Involves:	heart
Its nature is:	spiritual
It is:	giving

Scripture, the concept of love is **always** set forth as active. For example, when Jesus said, "Thou shalt love the Lord thy God with all thy heart" (Luke 10:27), the verb *to love* is in the active voice.

Jesus did not say, "Thou shalt *be in love with* the Lord thy God." That would not be active. Rather, He said, "Thou shalt *love* the Lord thy God." That is in the active voice. At no point in the Bible does it ever say, "Be in love." It always says, "Love." There is a world of difference.

In a later chapter we will look in some detail at Ephesians 5:25. There the Apostle Paul wrote, "Husbands, *love* your wives." He did not write, "Husbands, *be in love with* your wives." What the Scripture says here is in the active voice. Husbands are commanded of God to love their wives actively.

LOVE IS COMMANDED

This may seem like semantics, but there is a crucial point here. Let me illustrate it this way:

Over the years, I have had many a counseling situation with a couple when one or the other has said to me, "I just don't love him/her anymore." I have often been tempted to say, "Well, do you have any other sins you wish to confess?" Jesus said, "A new commandment I give unto you, That ye love one another; as I have loved you" (John 13:34). We are commanded of God to love one another, and that certainly involves our spouses.

The world has perpetrated the idea that *being in love* is a warm, fuzzy, romantic feeling which floats down upon us like some ethereal cloud. The idea is advanced that Cupid has shot his arrow and there is nothing we can do about it. It's kind of like catching a virus. The doctor cannot define it or treat it. All he knows is that you have it.

This author is not against people's "falling in love," but that kind of love does not sustain a marriage. Accordingly, I have had people over the years tell me, "I have fallen out of love with him/her."

Again, nowhere does the Bible speak of *falling into love* or of *being in love*. Rather, the clear command *to love* is repeated often. It is active. It is an imperative. It is something that we have control over. It is something at which we must continually work.

To love (in the *agape* sense) is to be kind. It is to be

sacrificial. It is to yield of oneself. It is to be considerate of the other. It is to be courteous. It is to be oriented toward the happiness of the other and not of oneself.

MATURITY

We touch here upon a related subject. That is the concept of maturity. As he has read the development of the principle of *agape* love in this chapter, some reader may think, *Hey, that's not for me. I want to do my own thing and seek my own interests. I mean, number one is what's most important to me.* That is a fairly good illustration of immaturity. Immature people are those who live for themselves. By contrast, maturity is to be others-oriented. Maturity is being selfless.

When our children were babies, they didn't care if they woke us up in the middle of the night. All they were interested in was what *they* wanted. It may have been a bottle. It may have been a diaper change. It may have been something else. But they cried and carried on. If poor old Mom or Dad was low on sleep or not feeling well, that was of little concern to them. They wanted "their thing," and they were going to carry on until they got it.

The children, when they were infants, were immature; but their mother was mature. In her love, she would get up and take care of her children. She loved them.

When the children were just a little older, they still didn't care if they caused extra work and headaches for their mother. If it was fun to tip a bowl of applesauce on their heads, they did it. But good old Mom would clean up the mess and clean them up. She loved them, and her maturity and love for her children caused her to give of herself willingly to clean up the messes.

Today, when home, our young adult daughters will look for ways to take some of the load off their mother. They may of their own initiative vacuum the house or do the laundry.

Because they have grown in love and maturity, they now seek to do things for their mother and help her.

Years ago when they were infants and toddlers, it was another story. Then, in their immaturity, all they were interested in was Mother's satisfying them. But now since they have become mature spiritually, they have grown to give of themselves for their mother.

However, patterns of immaturity carry over into many a marriage. Children grow up demanding and having their desires met. They grow up seeking self-gratification in one form or another. They become adults physically and enter into marriage, but the spiritual immaturity that has been the essence of their character continues on into their marriages. Therefore, once the honeymoon has passed, they revert back to the old habits of self-seeking and self-interest.

There is a direct parallel between immaturity and a lack of *agape* love. Conversely, there is a close parallel between *agape* love and genuine maturity. Both of the latter tend to be selfless. Because of this, I teach couples who claim to have "fallen out of love" with each other to work again at loving each other actively, on purpose, specifically.

Some have replied, "Well, he or she just is not very lov-

	IMMATURITY	MATURITY	
Selfishness	◄───────────────	──────────────►	Selflessness
	LACK OF AGAPE LOVE	AGAPE LOVE	

able anymore." That is beside the point. The Bible says that we are to love one another even as Christ loved us. The truth is, none of us was ever very lovable to God. The Scripture describes us as being enemies of God. We were rebellious and defiled before we were saved. "But God, who is rich in mercy, for his great love wherewith he loved us" (Eph. 2:4), has in His grace reached down and saved us. Just as God has graciously been willing to love and forgive us, so He commands that we are to love our spouses.

Some may protest, "But you don't know what she looks like now." Well, perhaps time and pounds have conspired together so that she is no longer a contestant for a beauty contest. The Bible says to love her anyway.

Someone else says, "But you don't know what he did." The Bible says to love him still. There is no question **there are many things which can take the blossom off the rose of a marriage, but a major restorative principle is to return to loving each other.** Do it on purpose. Initially, do it even mechanically if need be, but do it.

LOVE TENDS TO RECIPROCATE ITSELF

Others may reply, "Well, he or she will not come for counsel or read this book." Love him or her anyway. Genuine *agape* love has an amazing property. It tends to reciprocate itself. That is, genuine *agape* love will tend to return itself. It may not happen immediately; it may not come easily; but if practiced long enough and seriously enough, there will be a positive and pleasant harvest.

"We love him, because he first loved us" (I John 4:19). God has persevered in loving us, and we in due season have come to return love to Him. It did not come immediately nor consistently; but because God has maintained His love for us, we have come to love Him.

Agape love tends to return.

The same principle will tend to be true in a marriage relationship. Though one spouse may have grown cold and apart, if the other will diligently love that one and make it known in various ways, in due season there *very well may be* a reciprocation of that love.

It is fairly easy to take a large amount of cold water and put out the flames in a wood fire. And though it may not be as easy, it is possible to rekindle that fire.

We have a fire ring in our backyard. At times when we have had church fellowships or family gatherings, we have built a fire for roasting wieners or marshmallows. However, it seems the wood stacked there is always wet when we go to light the fire. It seems like it rains the day before every such planned activity. Getting a fire going under such circumstances is a chore, but it can be done. By kindling the wet wood with much dry newspaper and by pouring generous amounts of fuel oil on the pile, a fire can be ignited.

Unfortunately, when the fuel oil and paper are consumed, the rest of the pile of damp wood just sputters and smolders and if left alone will quickly die out. But then more fuel oil is added, and again the flames flare up. When the fuel oil has been consumed, the fire starts to die out again. So again more fuel oil is poured on the fire, and immediately the flames shoot up. But as the accelerant has been continually added, the fire has little by little become hot enough to take hold and sustain itself. We have done it many times. It works.

Likewise, in a marriage where there is a lack of *agape* love, the flame will fade out; but it can be rekindled. It will take time. It will take effort. It may mean a complete change in habits of the relationship. But if one party in a marriage will actively work at loving the other in a selfless way, the flame in the marriage can be rekindled.

Agape love is active, not passive. Just as it takes active effort to light a fire with damp wood and keep it burning, people can work at loving each other to the point where the fire finally takes hold and sustains itself.

LOVE IS KIND AND THOUGHTFUL

If there are two words which summarize the principle of *agape* love, they are *kindness* and *thoughtfulness*.

Kindness. First Corinthians 13:4 says, "*[Love]...is kind.*" Therefore, in developing *agape* love, kindness is paramount. Kindness is using soft words instead of sharp. Kindness is complimenting instead of criticizing. Kindness is being courteous rather than rude. Kindness is preparing what we know our spouse likes. Kindness is helping our spouse. Kindness is buying gifts for our spouse. Kindness is trying to make our spouse feel better. Kindness is seeking to lift the spirit of our spouse. Kindness is telling our spouse we are proud of him or her. Kindness is forgiving. Kindness is getting that little something to brighten the day of our spouse.

Kindness is:

- ❤ Using soft words instead of sharp
- ❤ Complimenting instead of criticizing
- ❤ Being courteous rather than rude
- ❤ Preparing what we know our spouse likes
- ❤ Helping our spouse
- ❤ Buying gifts for our spouse
- ❤ Trying to make our spouse feel better
- ❤ Seeking to lift the spirit of our spouse
- ❤ Telling our spouse we are proud of him of her
- ❤ Forgiving
- ❤ Getting that little something to brighten the day of our spouse

Thoughtfulness. Kindness is being thoughtful. Thoughtfulness is finding a way to make the load lighter for our spouse. Thoughtfulness is getting up early to make breakfast for your husband. Thoughtfulness is having his hunting clothes all washed and clean on hunting day. Thoughtfulness is making the pie he likes and putting a piece in his lunch. Thoughtfulness is buying a rose for your wife on the way home. Thoughtfulness is helping your wife with the dishes. Thoughtfulness is picking up your dirty clothes so your wife does not have to. Thoughtfulness is taking her out to eat so she does not have to prepare supper. Thoughtfulness is buying her the outfit she has been wanting. Thoughtfulness is getting the piece of hunting gear he has been wanting. Thoughtfulness is thinking about what will please your spouse, and doing it.

Thoughtfulness is:

- Finding a way to make the load lighter for our spouse
- Getting up early to make breakfast for your husband
- Having his hunting clothes all washed and clean on hunting day
- Making the pie he likes and putting a piece in his lunch
- Buying a rose for your wife on the way home
- Helping your wife with the dishes
- Picking up your dirty clothes so your wife does not have to
- Taking her out to eat so she does not have to prepare supper
- Buying her the outfit she has been wanting
- Thinking about what will please your spouse, and doing it

In these little scenarios the focus and emphases have been on thinking about and doing for the other. In none of these situations has the thought been of doing something or getting something for oneself. It is focused upon the one loved (or the person one is trying to love). *Agape* love is kindness. It is thoughtfulness.

Some perhaps are thinking, *Man, there will be no fun if I live that way. Everything is designed to make the other person happy.* The truth is, as we live to make the other person happy, the other person will tend to reciprocate. That is, sooner or later he or she will begin to behave similarly toward you.

Jesus said, "It is more blessed to give than to receive" (Acts 20:35). The happiest people in life are the givers; and without a doubt, the most miserable people in life are the "getters."

I have observed that even apart from any consequences relating to marriage, people who live for themselves are universally unhappy. This is in accordance with one of the great paradoxes of Christianity: Those who give of themselves for others are far happier than those who live for themselves.

Self-focused people invariably have problems with depression. They are usually in a huff at someone for something. Because they are selfish, they are not well liked by their peers. They pout and run around with hurt feelings. Whenever something does not go their way, they make a scene. They may complain they have few friends.

Watching the rich and famous in the world about us can be interesting. Not all are self-focused, but in my view, more fit that profile than not. Their drug and alcohol problems go along with their being self-focused. We read of their divorces. We read of their patronage of the psychologists and therapists. From time to time we read of their suicides.

Perhaps a classic illustration of utter misery is the modern British royal family. They have it all—wealth, fame, prestige, influence and virtually any material thing they want. Yet most of them are in a big mess in life. From what I have read, one thing seems clear for most of them: they are quite self-focused. Their problems are spiritual. For the most part, they have shown little or no *agape* love in their marriage relationships.

When self-focused people enter marriage, invariably they will continue their selfish lifestyle. For some reason, their parents allowed them to develop as selfish individuals. As elementary-aged children, they pursued doing what *they* wanted to do. As adolescents, the pattern continued and became entrenched in the very fabric of their character. As young adults, the distortion of selfishness twisted their personalities. They became sophisticated enough to put on a sweet and pleasant appearance when they wanted to impress.

That is what they did as they met their future spouses. But once courtship was completed and the honeymoon was over, the old pattern of life reemerged. The marriage of each such couple was bumpy from the first. One or both of them were self-focused. They tended to be unhappy individually; when they married, the conflict of their two self-focused personalities multiplied their unhappiness.

One might ask, "Can such a person change?" The answer is yes. However, the longer that pattern of life has been engrained, the harder it will be to change. But it can be done if one is willing to change.

An old saying is: "As the twig is bent, so grows the tree." On our property, there are hundreds, if not thousands, of trees. We live in Duluth, Minnesota, in the woods on the edge of town. Our city is nestled in the northern wilderness. Bears, deer, foxes, moose, lynx, eagles and wolves all visit our property.

I have been fascinated by the growth pattern of some of the trees on our property. Some have grown for decades at angles far less than vertical. Why they have, I don't know, but it is evident they have been in that situation for many years. Some have a contortion or unusual angle in their trunks. Whatever happened years ago, I will never know. By some means, when they were young and tender, their trunks were distorted. Another tree may have fallen against each. In any event, the character of the trunks of some trees is distorted.

How can such a tree be straightened? Well, certainly not easily. However, I have watched a neighbor up the road try to straighten a bent pine tree in his front yard. The tree had a bow in its trunk as it rose toward the sky. A much larger maple tree was not far away.

The neighbor took a come-along winch device and fastened one end to the trunk of the large maple tree. Then after having "padded" the bent pine tree at the appropriate place, he fastened the cable to it. He used the come-along winch to put tension on the cable. As it pulled against the large maple, the big tree did not move, but the bent pine tree was slowly straightened. Another year or two was necessary before the bow in the pine tree was completely pulled out, but it was gradually accomplished.

Likewise, when the character of one or both spouses has been distorted by a self-focused pattern of life, their marriage will not change overnight. However, with time and effort it can be corrected by the grace of God. It may not be easy, and there may be pressure in the doing of it. But if at least one party will begin to live for the other, giving of himself or herself, *agape* love will begin to work. *Agape* love will tend to reciprocate itself. Sooner or later, the recalcitrant spouse will begin to return the love.

LIVE FOR THE OTHER

For as long as I can remember, a little plaque has hung

in our home. I don't know where it came from or who wrote the words, but it certainly is true. It says, "Home is where each lives for the other and all live for Christ." Though that is not a verse of Scripture, it surely reflects a biblical philosophy. To live for the other is a manifestation of *agape* love. To live for the Lord is likewise an outworking of the principle of *agape* love.

Paul wrote in Philippians 2:3, "Let each esteem other better than themselves." The context there is not of marriage as such, but the principle certainly can apply. As each considers his spouse better than himself and so gives the other deference, a multitude of problems will be avoided.

When each esteems the other better than himself, he will live for the other. In the next verse, Paul wrote, "Look not every man on his own things, but every man also on the things of others." Again, the context is not dealing with marriage but is applicable to it. As we become more concerned about the needs and interests of our spouses than we are about our own interests, *agape* love will be in action.

"In honour preferring one another" (Rom. 12:10). That is an application of the principle of *agape* love. It suggests placing the other before oneself.

Indeed, *agape* love is putting our spouses ahead of ourselves. It is placing their interests ahead of our interests. It is buying for them before we buy for ourselves. It is doing what they want to do before we do what we want. It is yielding our wills to their wills.

Some may wonder how this last statement agrees with the biblical injunction for a wife to submit to her husband. We devote a considerable amount of space to that in a later chapter. Here, suffice it to say, the husband is the ultimate head of the home and must make the final decisions; but that does not exempt him from deferring to his wife in routine, day-to-day matters.

Likewise, she ought to defer to him. *Agape* love in marriage is not only *giving* of oneself *for* the other; it is also *yielding* oneself *to* the other. *Agape* love is more than just giving material things to our spouses: it also means yielding our wills.

Put your spouse ahead of yourself. Wife, yield to your husband; and, husband, yield to your wife in matters of day-to-day consequence. You will find as you give of yourself in every area of your life, your marriage will progressively become happier.

TWELVE PRINCIPLES EMANATING FROM *AGAPE* LOVE

In summary, we state twelve secondary principles which emanate from the primary principle of *agape* love in marriage:

1. Give in. If one is willing to give of himself for the other, then he should yield himself to his spouse in every legitimate concern.

The problem is, by nature we want our own way. Incidentally, giving in with a chip on your shoulder, in a pout or with a grudge, is not an outworking of *agape* love. Give in not only in deed but in attitude. Yield to the wishes of your spouse.

Now for this principle to be worked out successfully, **both** spouses must yield mutually. The problem comes when one in particular insists on his or her own way. Both need to yield to each other in routine, day-to-day matters.

2. Be kind. Always, always be kind! Even when everything else goes wrong, be kind. Work at it. Practice it. Think up ways to be kind.

Incidentally, most norms of courtesy and politeness are rooted in the more basic principle of being kind to one another. The most important person in your life is your spouse. Be kind to that one. Outlaw in your own person manifestations of unkindness that are even as common as sarcasm and a biting tongue. The greatest potential source of unkindness is the part of the human anatomy that resides between the teeth. Actively work at bridling your tongue.

3. Be selfless. That's more easily said than done. Our basic human nature is intrinsically selfish. But *agape* love is a giving of ourselves for others.

Work at pleasing your spouse. Practice it by buying for him or her. Think up little acts of kindness which you can do for him or her. Work at shaping yourself into the mold of living *for* your spouse.

Later we will consider the principle of crucifying self. Death is an excellent picture of what your relationship to your self-interests should be: you should be dead to your own interests and alive to the interests of your spouse.

4. Be thoughtful. Think of your spouse. Think of what might brighten his or her day. Think of how you can be helpful to him or her. Try to think of things that will encourage him or her. (Again, the focus is on the other and not on yourself.)

5. Be patient. The Scripture says that love is long-suffering (patient). Resist the urge to be upset with your spouse. The fact is, he or she may very likely be having a difficult day or be under pressure from problems of life. Think about your spouse's situation and don't allow yourself the liberty of venting your frustrations.

6. Do not erupt. Control your temper. Control negative emotions such as jealousy, envy, anger and bitterness. *Agape* love will mitigate your displeasure when you stop to consider that your spouse makes the same mistakes *you* do.

7. Place the other ahead of yourself. Defer to the wishes of your spouse. Though the husband is ultimately the head of the household, in routine, day-to-day transactions in the home, put your spouse ahead of yourself.

8. Be faithful. Adultery is wrong morally. In addition to that fact, it is catastrophically disruptive to a marriage. On a personal basis, *agape* love will cause a person to consider how devastating infidelity will be to a spouse. If there were no deterrent besides *agape* love, it alone would preclude any infidelity.

9. Resist irritation. Life is full of irritants. When two people live side by side in a marriage relationship, little quirks may irritate one another. *Agape* love will cause us to overlook those irritants and give up our irritation toward our spouse. (This is not to say we should not talk about the irritant at some appropriate time. We will discuss that in a later chapter.)

10. Overlook faults. We all have shortcomings and flaws in our lives. The problem is, we readily see the faults in our spouses but are oblivious to our own. *Agape* love will overlook the faults in a spouse. (Again, that is not to say at the appropriate time and in the proper manner the fault should not be discussed.)

11. Put up with incidentals. I know that sounds very clichéd. However, if we are willing to give of ourselves for our mates, then we will accept situations that may be less than ideal because we love our spouses.

Of course, this is within the boundaries of righteousness and propriety. The Apostle Paul wrote, "That your love may abound yet more and more in knowledge and in all judgment" (Phil. 1:9). Paul is saying that our love ought to have boundaries, even as a river has banks. The boundaries of our love are knowledge and good judgment—or reduced to even simpler terms, they are what is right. Propriety and what is right form the boundaries of the giving of ourselves in *agape* love.

12. Seek what is right. First Corinthians 13 says that love rejoices in truth and not in iniquity. As we will see in a coming chapter, righteousness will prevent and solve a multitude of problems.

First Corinthians 13 concludes, "The greatest of these is charity [love]." Love is the first major principle within a marriage relationship. The highest form is *agape* love. It will preclude and solve a multitude of sins. "Charity [love] shall cover the multitude of sins" (I Pet. 4:8). *Agape* love will solve a multitude of problems in your marriage.

If you learn nothing else from this book, learn to develop *agape* love in your marriage. It will make a profound difference.

5.

PHILEO LOVE

NUANCES OF *PHILEO*

In the last chapter, we touched upon how there are several types of love found in the Greek words translated "love." The first of these is *agape* and is detailed in the preceding chapter. In the New Testament, the Holy Spirit used another word which is translated "love." This is *phileo* (pronounced "fil-*ay*-oh"). In this chapter, we will discuss this *phileo* love.

For about every five mentions of the word *agape* in the New Testament, the word *phileo* is mentioned only once. That should give some perspective of the importance the Holy Spirit has given to *agape* love. Nevertheless, *phileo* love is an important part of the foundation of a strong marriage. It certainly is a necessary ingredient for a marriage which is to be heaven on earth.

Before we delve into the applications of this concept, let us look at the etymology of the word and its nuances. On its simplest and lowest level, the word *phileo* is used to mean "like." For example, Jesus said that the hypocrites "love to pray standing in the synagogues and in the corners of the streets" (Matt. 6:5). Here the context indicates that the hypocrites *liked* so to pray.

A higher sense of the word is of "enjoying" something or someone. Jesus spoke of the scribes who "love greetings in the markets, and the highest seats in the synagogues" (Luke 20:46). The scribes *enjoyed* their social standing.

An even higher sense of the word is that of "fellowship." "The Father loveth the Son, and sheweth him all things that himself doeth" (John 5:20). Though it is certain God the Father loves the Son in an *agape* sense (John 3:35), in John 5:20 the word *phileo* is used. The context indicates *fellowship* between the Father and the Son.

"He whom thou lovest is sick" (John 11:3). Here again the word *phileo* is used in reference to the *friendship* which Jesus had with Lazarus.

All things being equal, the word *phileo* probably refers to friendship more than it does to anything else. Jesus wept over Lazarus' death, and the Jews commented, "Behold how he loved him!" (John 11:36). Here the word *phileo* evidently has the sense of close friendship.

It is of further interest that, on occasion, the words *agape* and *phileo* are used almost interchangeably in two statements concerning a similar Bible teaching (such as in Revelation 3:19 and Hebrews 12:6). In its highest sense, *phileo* approaches *agape* love.

To summarize, *phileo* love conveys a continuum of meaning ranging from liking or enjoying someone or something, to having a sense of fellowship with someone, to friendship, to close friendship that approaches *agape* love. In a nutshell, it might best be summarized by the idea of *friendship*.

So we come to the matter of friendship within a marriage. That might sound odd, but there are marriages where the partners are barely friends. They share the same house and the same bed but are not close friends.

PHILEO LOVE
Friendship; sharing

AGAPE LOVE
God's love; giving

EROS LOVE
Physical; receiving

Before further developing the idea of *phileo* love in marriage, let us relate the matter of friendship to our total being. *Agape* love emanates from the heart and is therefore spiritual. *Eros* love pertains largely to the body and is therefore physical. Friendship is not necessarily spiritual nor physical. Rather, it pertains more to our intellectual, social and communicative interests. It emanates from the psyche (mind) and is therefore largely mental.

We might organize the concepts as follows:

Type of love:	*agape*
Involves:	heart
Its nature is:	spiritual
It is:	giving
Type of love:	*phileo*
Involves:	mind
Its nature is:	mental
It is:	sharing

Through this quarter of a century, my wife has been my best friend. I think she certainly would concur and eagerly agree that the feeling is mutual. We each have other friends, both individually and mutually, but our closest friendship has been between ourselves.

FRIENDSHIP

What forms the basis of a friendship? There are no doubt several factors. Let me mention some:

Perhaps the most common denominator of friendship is the sharing of the same interests. When two people who have common interests meet, a potential for friendship exists.

Let me illustrate. I make no apology for being a conservative in almost every sense of the word. As a result, I have had occasion to meet other people who are conservatives. In particular I have gotten to know one couple in our community who share much the same philosophy and convictions which I hold. Therefore, there is a common denominator between them and me. I don't often go to political meetings; but when I do, we sit together, because: (a) we know each other; (b) we share the same interests; and (c) we enjoy each other's company. As a result, (d) we have fellowship together, and (e) we have worked on projects together. I consider them my friends.

Because I am a pastor, I recently received a long-distance phone call from a man I have never met nor even heard of. He was a missionary candidate seeking to speak in our church. As the conversation progressed, comment was made that the city where we live is a seaport on the Great Lakes. He told me he was from Cleveland, Ohio and that his hobby was watching the ships come and go from various ports on the shores of Lake Erie. We then began to talk about the shipping traffic where I live in Duluth. I too have an interest in watching the ships come and go.

The conversation became more animated as we talked about a shared interest. He had never been to Duluth, which is the largest seaport on the Great Lakes, but he was interested in the unique circumstances surrounding this port. During a few minutes of spontaneous conversation, we who had been strangers became friends because of a shared interest. There was instant fellowship, and a fledgling friendship was born. Our mutual interests drew us together.

Now let us focus on marriage. In several stereotypical situations the honeymoon has been over for a long time because there is no real sense of friendship in the marriages. Let me describe such a scenario.

Bob and Jill were married. To a degree they loved each

other, but their marriage was almost like living in a boardinghouse. He went his way, and she went hers. For years Bob had an interest in restoring old cars. There was always an old clunker parked in the garage or behind the house. Each Saturday Bob watched a program on public TV about car restoration. He periodically went to car shows where restored cars were displayed, bought and sold. He subscribed to periodicals on restoring old cars. As time and money allowed, he spent much energy out in the garage gradually restoring an old '52 Chevy and a '54 Plymouth. He was proud of his work.

In the summer when the streets were dry, he took his latest re-creation out to tool around town on a soft evening.

But Jill couldn't care less about cars. To her a car was a car. Once you'd seen one, you'd seen them all. A car was just a vehicle to get her from Point A to Point B. She had no interest in Bob's old cars. She wouldn't go to the car shows with him. She wouldn't help him on his restorations, even when they involved sewing fabric for the upholstery. When he went out for his little jaunts in the summer in his latest restored car, she would not go. Why waste the time?

Rather, her interest was Siamese cats. She had two, and she fussed over them continually. She read everything she could about Siamese. From time to time she went to the cat shows in the region. She had little cat figurines around the house. The highlights of her year were the several cat shows in which she could show her favorite Siamese cat.

So Bob went his way and messed with his cars, and Jill went her way and did her cat things. Though they did not fight much, Bob and Jill's marriage was cool and thin and certainly not close. Their children had left home. Probably the only thing keeping them together was the financial advantages of being married. Though their marriage was not hell on earth, it certainly was not heaven on earth.

Their problem was that they shared few common interests. Consequently, they did not have a great degree of fellowship, and they didn't do much together. There was not a great depth of *phileo* love in their marriage. In a limited sense, they were friends; but as far as closeness and intimacy of fellowship were concerned, they were rather lean.

There are variations of this problem all over the country. The details will be different, but distance between the partners exists for the same reason—lack of friendship.

Moreover, such situations give the Devil opportunity to tempt by means of the opposite sex. Strong *agape* love and *phileo* love form the basis for the fullest degree of *eros* love or sexual intimacy. When a couple is shallow or cool in their nonphysical relationships, they will not have the degree of physical intimacy and pleasure of a couple who are deeply committed to each other and are best of friends. This creates a weak link which the Devil may exploit through someone else. Because a couple's physical intimacy is in a low orbit, a third party who creates a spark of infatuation can lead to serious trouble.

WHAT SAITH THE SCRIPTURES?

Rather than trying to figure out who is wrong in marriages with low friendship levels, let's go to the Scripture and find a solution to the problem. The Apostle Paul wrote, "That they may teach the young women...to love their husbands" (Titus 2:4). The word used here is *philandros*. This word consists of the prefix *phil*, which is the root word of *phileo*, and *andros*, which is the basic root word for *husband*. If we follow the development of the idea as outlined above, this verse essentially teaches that the *wife* ought to be a friend to her husband. It is the wife who is to share the interests of her husband, and not the other way around.

Curiously, there is no corresponding verse in the Bible which teaches the husband to be a friend of the wife. That is not to say a husband ought not to be a friend to his wife, but the imperative of the Scripture is for the wife to take the initiative in sharing her husband's interests. In a later chapter we will see that husbands are commanded to love their wives. However, the word used in that command is *agape*.

In the stereotypical story of Bob and Jill sketched above, it was Jill who should have taken the time and effort to share Bob's interests. The closeness and intimacy of their relationship could have increased if she had become involved in Bob's interests. Having it the other way around would not necessarily solve the problem.

In this day of radical feminism and "political correctness," what you have just read is utter heresy and blasphemy for some; but it is rooted in biblical principle. However, most couples having a similar problem should not trace its root to feminism or "political correctness." The statement of their problem is much more prosaic than that: there is often a wife who is *unwilling to give of herself* to share in her husband's interests. (We are now very close to where we were a chapter ago in discussing *agape* love.) The Bible teaches it is the wife who is to adjust and modify her life for her husband, and not the other way around.

As I commented earlier, our marriage has been a taste of Heaven on earth. I have often jokingly said, "It's all my wife's fault." Pam has always been willing to follow her husband and make herself interested in his pursuits.

There have been several occasions over the years in which I related to her that I felt the Lord was leading me to another place. She is the type of person who makes her home where she is. Frankly, on a personal level, she was not thrilled with the prospect of moving; but her attitude has always been, "Honey, if this is what the Lord is leading you to do, I am with you all the way." And she has been just that.

On a more mundane level, Pam has always been willing to become engaged in my interests. She has sought to conform her pursuits to mine. Therefore, (1) we have not fussed over who was going to do what, and (2) we have had intimacy of fellowship because she became interested in what I was interested in. As a result, we have been best of friends over these years.

In the early years of the ministry, when I was a youth pastor, she eagerly became interested in youth work. When a significant portion of my ministry pertained to church Sunday school bus ministries, she willingly became a Sunday school bus worker. When the Lord placed me into a senior pastorate, she willingly became the pastor's wife with all of its entertaining and pressures. When the Lord led me to start a church "from scratch," she willingly went to work to help support the family.

On a personal level, if I took an interest in some pursuit, she willingly went along. As I have said, I love to go down to the harbor area here in Duluth and watch the ships at this Great Lakes seaport. There is a museum explaining the history of the region and of Great Lakes shipping. Though we have been there often, she is always willing to go with me yet another time to see the museum or to watch a ship. I think Pam personally cares little about ships and their lore. But she has willingly conformed her interests to those of her husband. Though this certainly is not a big part of our lives, she willingly seeks to go where her husband goes and to be interested in what he is interested in. As a result, we are best of friends.

I have an interest in aircraft. I do not fly, but the little boy in me has always liked airplanes. About every other summer there is a major air show in our community. Various aircraft from around the world are brought in for flight and ground display shows. I usually try to attend.

To Pam, an airplane is an airplane; if you have seen one, you have seen them all. But every other year she *willingly* goes with me to the air show. She is willing to form her interests around those of her husband. She desires to be with her husband and go where he goes and do what he does, and she never complains about it.

For years I have had an interest in military equipment. Therefore, when there are military displays or programs in the area, she willingly tags along with her husband to see them. When the U.S. Navy brings a warship into port as a public relations exercise, Pam willingly goes along with her husband to tour it. I don't think she is all that interested in the ship itself, but she seeks to become interested in what her husband finds of interest.

Our daughters attended Pensacola Christian College in Pensacola, Florida. There are major military sites in the Pensacola area, not the least of which is the Naval Air Museum. Pam has gone with me to the museum more than once. She seeks to be interested in what her husband is interested in. There are other historic military sites in the area, dating from the Civil War era. Again, she *willingly* goes along to tour these sites and becomes interested along with me.

The point of this discussion is, my wife and I are best friends. We share many things of mutual interest, but above and beyond that, Pam willingly seeks to conform her interests to those of her husband. Therefore, we have a rich reservoir of common interests as a basis of fellowship and enjoyment.

As our friendship has grown deeper, so has our love, particularly mine for her. She lives for her husband. How can I not love her more and more? Our lives are one. We are one spirit, one mind and one flesh. A major key to that is that Pam *willingly* seeks to share her husband's interests. Therefore, our friendship continues to grow.

To summarize this point, Titus 2:4 says the wife is to love her husband. The word is *philandros* and literally means "to be a friend to her husband." Friendship is based upon a sharing of interests, which leads to personal fellowship. The fellowship of personal friendship is a building block that forms the foundation of a strong marriage.

COMMUNICATION

Another factor which is critical in friendship between a husband and a wife is communication. It is the stuff of which fellowship is built. Without a doubt, a major source of stress in many marriages is a lack of communication.

Let me digress to share a story which illustrates the point. While at college, one of my young adult daughters gained a gentleman friend. In fact, they became *close* friends. Every time we talked to her, it was "John this" and "John that" (not his real name). Whenever she got around to writing to us, she seasoned her letters with news about John.

Well, summer came, and both went their ways. John lived a thousand miles away. Because of this, they were separated for the summer. To make matters worse, they were not exactly the world's greatest letter writers, and they did not write as much as they could have. By the time they went back to school in the fall, their friendship had faded.

PHILEO LOVE
⇓
Friendship
⇓
Fellowship
⇓
Communication
⇓
Problem Resolution

There were no "third parties" involved. They just had not communicated a great deal over the summer, and because the communication was weak, the friendship fizzled out. Sadly, the same often happens in a marriage.

Not only is fellowship based upon communication, it is also based upon resolving problems. That depends to a large extent upon communicating. It seems people go to extremes and at times do not find a happy medium in communicating with each other. On the one hand is the extreme of not talking about problems. On the other is the extreme of exploding at each other. Both are wrong, and both are destructive. We cannot ignore problems, yet we cannot explode at each other in trying to deal with problems.

Certainly not all couples are alike, and there are more than just two personality types; but it seems that frequently a couple is made up of one partner who tends to be reserved and the other who tends to be the opposite. Men often tend to be reserved, and women often tend to be loquacious. Sometimes it is the other way around; but for the sake of our discussion, we will proceed with that stereotype.

In many a home when there are problems or difficulties, the man will tend to bury the problem, and the woman will tend to blow her stack. This often causes the husband to crawl deeper into his shell and only adds more frustration to the wife who in turn vents it on her husband. In such a stereotypical situation, both parties are wrong. By burying the problem, the husband is not communicating to resolve it. However, in slashing away with her tongue, the wife is only exacerbating whatever the problem may be.

TALK ABOUT PROBLEMS

A critical means to keep a strong friendship is to communicate about your problems. Learn to deal with irritations. The truth is, two people living in an environment as close as marriage will irritate each other from time to time. Each individual came from a different family background. Families do things differently.

For example, a husband may have come from a home where it was acceptable for the man to leave his wet towels and washcloths on the floor. So the young husband does the same to his bride. However, she came from a home where her mother insisted her father pick up after himself. Her husband's sloppiness irritates her. That irritation, coupled with other irritants, leads to fussing, nagging and fighting. As they argue over little irritations, the close fellowship they had before they were married becomes strained.

(Apart from communicating about the irritation, the husband here should have had the maturity not to leave a mess for his wife. This is especially true if he perceived that she was irritated by it. *Agape* love will go a long way in solving such conflicts. In any event, they need to sit down and talk about the problem.)

A major bone of contention in many a marriage concerns who will spend what for whom. A variation of that theme is that one or the other goes ahead and buys something. Then conflict arises over paying the bills. From such conflict, heated arguments may arise. Bitterness and frustration may develop, and the fellowship of friendship is eroded. Conflict over money and how it is spent probably dilutes and destroys more *phileo* love than any other single matter. Communication about money matters needs to be careful and clear.

Chuck represents a stereotypical husband in many a home. His wife, Sue, is a good woman and tries to please her husband. But when Sue doesn't iron his shirts just the way he likes them, it irritates Chuck. He doesn't say anything about it, but he doesn't forget it either.

He also likes his eggs turned just right, and if Sue fails to flip them that way, he sulks about it. If the car is parked a little askew in the garage, he grumbles about it to himself but not to Sue.

After awhile the irritations cause him to be in a snit against Sue. He becomes sullen toward her. He ignores her. He is crabby to her. Finally it all comes out in a big scene. Sue is frustrated with him because he often won't tell her what is bothering him. She is even more frustrated by the pettiness of the issues. Their fellowship and friendship are strained because of their communication bottlenecks. Marriage for them is not heaven on earth.

PRINCIPLES OF COMMUNICATION

Let us talk about several principles which are important in adequate communication concerning irritations and conflicts.

❶ Timing: *When* we sit down to talk is almost as important as *what* we will talk about and *how* we go about it. The temptation is to bring up the problem when your spouse walks in the door. At times a wife will hurl something at her husband right after he gets home from work. (The reverse can be just the same for a working wife.) He had hassles at work that day. Traffic was bad coming home. He has a headache. He's hungry. He's hot and sweaty. He has other problems on his mind.

When he walks in the house, the dog begins wagging its tail, and his wife begins wagging her tongue. Whatever the problem, that is not the time to deal with it.

Some forethought and consideration for the other spouse certainly are in order. After supper is over and he has had a chance to refresh himself may be a much better time to sit down and talk about whatever the problem is. Be thoughtful and considerate of your spouse in choosing the time to talk.

❷ Privacy: Never talk about personal problems in front of others. Don't do it in front of in-laws. Don't do it in front of the children. Don't do it in front of friends. If necessary, wait until after the children have gone to bed or, as an alternative, either send them to their rooms or go to your room and talk privately.

Over the years I have been amazed that couples air their problems in front of the children or other family members. That sort of thing does little to build personal fellowship and friendship between husband and wife.

❸ **Proportion:** Be careful you are not continually talking about problems. If there are several things which need to be talked about, prioritize the list. Deal with the most important things, but make sure there is plenty of pleasant conversation and fellowship between sessions of dealing with problems. Always seek to have more times of pleasant fellowship than troubleshooting times. Discussion of problems is important and most helpful, but it is also stressful. Intersperse times of good fellowship between times of dealing with problems.

❹ **Kindness:** Always be kind to each other as you discuss your conflicts or difficulties. Always! Remember, *agape* love is kind. The temptation will be present to get in a dig or to leave a little barb with the tongue. Make it a cardinal rule of your marriage always to be kind to your spouse—always.

Paul wrote to the Ephesian church of "speaking the truth in love" (Eph. 4:15). That means to say whatever has to be said in a kind way. You might even have to take time to figure out ahead of time a kind way to say what needs to be said.

❺ **Never lose your temper:** At times that is not easy. Through years of bad habit, some instinctively "blow their tops" when things go wrong. Anger is a normal human emotion, but it is a dangerous emotion. If we are not very careful, we will lose our tempers. When that happens, things come out which are wrong and hurtful.

I cannot remember a time in all of the years my wife and I have been married when either of us has lost his/her temper at the other. That is not to say it has not ever happened: I just do not remember it. Before you consider us abnormal people, let me hasten to say, we certainly have been tempted to lose our tempers; but by God's grace, we have not made any practice of it.

Some might protest that losing one's temper is typical of people from a given ethnic heritage. No doubt there are some ethnic backgrounds which contribute to a propensity toward emotional outbursts; but loss of temper, whether by habit or heritage, is never right. Over the years in counseling situations people have protested to me, "Well, that's just the way I am." My rejoinder to that excuse is, "Then change."

As children, we all heard the little ditty, "Sticks and stones may break my bones, but words will never hurt me." That might well be a little cultural device to deflect the sting of nasty words, but in reality it is not true. Words can cause deep emotional wounds. The nastiness which emanates from loss of temper has produced wounds which long have damaged the fellowship and potential friendship in many a marriage. Never lose your temper at your spouse!

I think of several situations I have known. The stereotype is something like this: Carol, the wife, had a tongue and a temper which could be likened to a howitzer and the projectile it fires. Over the years her marriage to Fred was rocky. When things went wrong, she would load up the old howitzer of her temper with choice words and blast them at her husband. A firefight would erupt as each shot repeatedly at the other.

Finally, things would simmer down, and after several hours they would apologize to each other; but Fred was never quite sure when Carol's cannon was going to go off again. Therefore, he always took overtime when it was offered at work and did not spend any more time at home than necessary. Their marriage continued, but it resembled life about three floors above purgatory. There was not a very strong degree of *phileo* love in their marriage. Though they had been married for years, close fellowship was virtually nonexistent in their home.

TALK ABOUT IT

To build *phileo* love, learn to fellowship with each other. Talk about keeping lines of communication open. Set times just to sit down and talk. Work at becoming best friends.

Listed below are things which will help develop friendship and keep conversations going. In fact, these things *should* be talked about on a somewhat regular basis:

① **Talk about finances.** Somebody needs to keep accurate, up-to-date records of the finances in your home. Whoever takes care of the checkbook and paying the bills should always share that information with the other spouse. Keeping the other informed about the general state of your affairs can prevent disaster later.

Always discuss any out-of-the-ordinary purchase with your spouse before going ahead with it. As mentioned in the preceding chapter, *agape* love will preclude selfishness of spending. Talking about prospective purchases beforehand will be thoughtful conversation. If your spouse is uneasy about a purchase, it is better to find out ahead of time than to find out afterward. Then you are stuck with not only a controversial purchase but a battle at home as well. Half the fun of buying something is knowing your spouse is on the same wavelength as you on the project; and a purchase without your spouse's approval will not be a happy purchase, even if you get your way.

Actually, talking about a purchase ahead of time and

thoughtfully hashing out the pros and cons can draw you closer to each other because of the opening up of yourself to your spouse. Rather than fighting over whether to buy something, make it a focal point for good conversation.

A husband who brings up the fact that he is the head of the house and doesn't need his wife's approval might be technically correct; but a husband who operates that way very long will be an unhappy camper, as will his wife. She will invariably feel her husband does not trust her judgment enough to seek her counsel. Furthermore, she may, with justification, feel that he is sneaking around behind her back to satisfy his selfish desires.

None of that is healthy for a marriage and certainly does not draw the partners into a deeper *phileo* love or friendship. A wise husband will counsel with his wife about any out-of-the-ordinary purchase. Not only will this head off a potential fight after he brings the item home, but it will build trust and fellowship for a closer friendship with his wife.

The same goes for the wife. Talk about finances and especially your intended purchases. More couples fight over money than any other one thing. Accordingly, more marriages end up in divorce over the handling of money than for any other reason.

②Talk about aggravations. When something your spouse does tends to irritate or aggravate you, sit down and talk about it. Do it kindly. Do it privately. Do it with your temper and tongue under control. Do it at an appropriate time. But do it.

You might want to broach the subject by saying, "Honey, can I talk to you about something? You may not realize it, but lately you always seem to leave your dirty clothes on the floor. It really bothers me. Would you mind picking them up and putting them into the laundry basket for me? It would really help me." Make sure the tone is sweet and no sarcasm or digs leak out.

Talking about an irritation may shed light on a subject you did not otherwise understand. If done in a pleasant manner, the very bringing up of the aggravation can lead to a good discussion which is helpful to building greater fellowship.

For example, your credit card bill arrives, and you notice there is a purchase at the local department store last month. The first thought is, your wife has gone and blown some money on some clothes she doesn't need. You are aggravated. But what you do not stop to think about is that she has in fact bought a Christmas gift early for one of the children.

The husband could holler, "What are you doing, spending all of our money again at the store?" Of course, that would probably engender a less than pleasant discussion. Or he could say, "Honey, I noticed on the credit card bill we spent $43.95 at the store last month. I need to know where to account for that in our budget." She then would explain what it was for, and the aggravation would probably be cleared up.

Talk about your aggravations. Do it kindly, privately and appropriately.

③ **Talk about what happened today.** Make time each day to talk about what went on at home or at work while the other was away. It may be mundane, but let your spouse know what you did. Then be willing to listen to the mundane details of your spouse's daily journey. That's what friends do.

Talk about the little things that happened at home with the children. Talk about the little incident which took place at work. Let your spouse be a part of the little things in your life. Keep your heart and your mind transparent to your spouse. Unless there is a legitimate reason for secrecy, like a surprise party, a birthday purchase or a company policy which forbids discussion, tell your spouse all you know. Just talk about things as time and situation allow. This is the stuff of which the friendship of *phileo* love is built. It is sharing your heart in the little details of day-to-day life.

④ **Talk about the children.** Children are of mutual concern to both parents, and both love them alike. Again, unless there is legitimate cause to withhold information from your spouse about your children (such as gifts purchased for the other parent), communicate to your spouse about the children. If you cannot think of anything else to talk about, you can usually talk about them. Share the high points and the problems in their lives. There is a rich source of fellowship and friendship in talking about children and their lives.

⑤ **Share family and neighborhood news.** As routine as it may seem, when you are aware of things in the neighborhood or your greater family, talk to your spouse about them. Not only are you being transparent in sharing what you know, but this is also a good forum for building friendship. (By the way, husbands, you may not always be interested in all of the little tidbits of in-law news, but be a good listener. Friendship at times means listening to things which are not absolutely thrilling to you.)

⑥ **Talk about vacation plans.** Everyone likes to take a vacation. (By the way, take your vacations together. It may be a fad of the day for husband and wife to "do their own thing" on vacation; but as a general rule, vacation together. That is not to preclude the husband's taking off occasionally on a fishing or hunting trip or the wife's attending a Christian ladies' retreat, but try to spend the rest of your vacation time as a couple.) Talk about it. Share plans. Be willing to bend as to where your spouse may be interested in going and what he/she may want to do.

The irony is, for some couples vacation is a negative

time because their spouses insist on doing certain things, and there is little discussion about it. Not only will you preclude hassles by talking about your vacations long in advance, but you will also have a potentially fun thing to build friendship around.

⑦ **Talk about physical intimacy.** You are married adults. You are legitimately sexually active to one degree or another. Talk about it (of course, privately, at the appropriate time and place). Discussing your interests or problems can enhance your physical love. It also can be a source for further development of friendship. There are few things of more personal intimacy in life than talking about such interests with your spouse. For a married couple, it is not only appropriate, it can also be a source for even greater *phileo* and *agape* love.

⑧ **Talk about your recreation interests.** The Bible teaches that the *wife* is to work at being a friend to her husband. This means she should become interested in his interests. (That is not to say the husband ought not to consider his wife's interests in this regard, but God has designated the husband to be the pacesetter of the home.)

I think much fellowship and friendship can be developed as a couple talk together about a given recreational or hobby interest. This may mean one party (the wife) becoming interested in a given pursuit; but by talking about the matter, interest will grow, and the fellowship will grow accordingly.

⑨ **Talk about weekly plans together.** Keep each other informed of family and personal schedules. We live in a hectic world. Talking about schedules ahead of time will not only keep everybody on the same frequency, but it will also be good for building friendship. Few things are more aggravating than finding out just ahead of an event that we are supposed to do a certain thing. What is even more aggravating is that our spouse "forgot" to tell us. Talk about plans, schedules and doings that involve anybody in the family.

⑩ **Apologize and ask forgiveness as necessary.** One of the hardest things in life to admit openly is "I was wrong," especially if there has already been some friction over a given matter. One of the first steps to reconciliation of a conflict is *confession.* Apart from any theological implications of this word, it means to own up to the wrong. To confess is to say, "I did it. I admit it. I was wrong."

Second, there is *contrition.* Again, apart from any theological overtone to that term, it means to be genuinely sorry.

To admit a wrong and to be sorry for it necessitate a humbling of ourselves. One reason people will not own up to a fault is pride. Pride and stubbornness prevent many from ever reconciling problems. (Incidentally, pride and stubbornness are essentially spiritual problems. They emanate from the human heart and pertain to our will.) To apologize genuinely is an act of virtue.

It is also a paradox of life. Though it involves humbling ourselves, apologizing does not make us smaller in the other's eyes. To the contrary, it makes us seem bigger and better. Our spouse already knows we were wrong. To deny our wrong only adds the negatives of stubbornness and pride to the mix of irritants. A contrite apology is a very healthy thing for a friendship.

Then there is the *asking of forgiveness.* To admit wrong and apologize contritely are good, but the final step is to ask forgiveness. The admission of fault on your part will help dissolve the problem in *your* heart. The granting of forgiveness by your spouse will release any animosity or barrier in *his* or *her* heart. (All things being equal, a timely apology and request for forgiveness will usually bring the desired forgiveness. If a spouse will not forgive, it is time to seek counseling.)

The failure to (1) admit fault, (2) apologize and (3) ask forgiveness can create a major barrier to further fellowship and friendship. Moreover, the side effects of failing to address offenses by either party can lead to bitterness and long-term damage to your relationship. Always be ready to apologize and seek or grant forgiveness. It is a crucial factor in keeping open the lines of communication and in developing the friendship of *phileo* love in your marriage.

```
STEPS TO RECONCILIATION

1. Confess

2. Apologize

3. Ask forgiveness
```

All of these are suggestions to increase communication within a marriage. Communication, once again, is the stuff of which fellowship is built. Fellowship is the precursor to friendship. *Phileo* love is essentially friendship. Make your spouse your best friend. Then build that *phileo* friendship to a personal intimacy which causes you to be one not only in body but also in mind and spirit.

* * *

We have gone into a considerable amount of discussion of the two basic types of love found in the New Testament. Let us also look very briefly at the other form—*eros* love. The Greek word *eros* does not appear in the Greek New Testament. However, it is a term from Greek heritage pertaining to sexual love. Though this word does not appear in the Bible per se, the concept certainly does. The modern English word *erotic* is derived from *eros*. As *agape* love pertains to our heart and is spiritual, and as *phileo* love pertains to the fellowship of friendship and hence is mental, so *eros* love pertains to our bodies and is physical.

Type of love:	agape
Involves:	heart
Its nature is:	spiritual
It is:	giving
Type of love:	phileo
Involves:	mind
Its nature is:	mental
It is:	sharing
Type of love:	eros
Involves:	body
Its nature is:	physical
It is:	receiving

We will not in this book further discuss *eros* love. However, from the chart above, you can see the relationship it has in the totality of human marriage.

6.

RIGHTEOUSNESS

INFRASTRUCTURE

As we continue to deal with foundational principles for a marriage which is heaven on earth, we come to a concept which at first may not seem to be particularly related to the matter of marriage and its happiness. Yet the principle of righteousness is truly part of the infrastructure of a heavenly marriage. Infrastructures are for the most part unnoticed yet are crucial to life functions. Righteousness is such a quality.

RIGHTEOUSNESS RIGHTEOUSNESS

R I G H T E O U S N E S S

R I G H T E O U S N E S S

RIGHTEOUSNESS

Heavenly Marriage Infrastructure

There are certain things in your home which are a part of its infrastructure, making it a pleasant place in which to live. Most people take their furnaces or air conditioning for granted—until it does not function properly. The foundation of the house is taken for granted until there is a problem with it. Perhaps more than anything else, the sewer system of your home is a part of its infrastructure which no one thinks about until it doesn't work. Just as a malfunctioning sewer can cause real problems, so a couple who do not have the character of righteousness in their marriage will have real problems. Moreover, they will be unhappy.

Righteousness is simply doing what is right. It means doing what I *ought* to do rather than doing what I *feel* like doing. In this sense, it is selfless; therefore, it is related to *agape* love.

We have already discussed *agape* love. Since righteousness is related to *agape* love, our separate study of righteousness may seem to be repetitive. Nevertheless, let us, by studying righteousness, look at the human heart and its relationship to others from a slightly different perspective.

Righteousness, as it pertains to a marriage, is doing what is right by one's spouse. It may not seem glamorous nor romantic; but let me assure you, it is part of the infrastructure of marriage. When righteousness toward a spouse is omitted, there will be all sorts of problems.

The Bible shows that righteousness is important in marriage because it brings peace. "And the work of righteousness shall be peace; and the effect of righteousness quietness and assurance for ever" (Isa. 32:17). The result of doing what is right is peace. As we continue to do what is right, there will be tranquillity and assurance. The word translated "assurance" has the sense of security or stability. Hence, doing what is right will bring not only peace but also stability and security to a given situation.

In applying this to a marriage relationship, the implications are profound. When a spouse does right by his or her mate, there will be peace between them. Conversely, when an individual does not do right by someone, there invariably will be friction. Unrighteousness causes trouble. If I don't do what is right by my spouse, there will not be the peace we could have had.

For example, suppose my wife has asked me repeatedly to take my dirty shoes off when I come into the house. If I leave them on anyway, what will happen? At the very least, there is going to be a reaction on her part. She may become angry. She may be hurt that I ignore her wishes. She may speak her mind. She may clam up and stew about it. She may blow her top. But the inevitable result will be that the tranquillity between us will become strained. She will be unhappy about the whole thing; eventually, so will I.

Let us suppose that family finances are in a jam. Therefore, the husband asks his wife not to use the credit card for anything other than an absolute emergency. However, when she goes shopping the next week, she sees a beautiful dress at the mall. She buys it and puts it on the credit card. (To excuse herself, she might make up some rationalization that she is a part of the family too and she deserves to indulge herself.) She goes home, hides the dress, and hopes her husband doesn't find out about it. Her little plan is to pull it out of the closet several months later and tell her husband that she has had that dress for a long time.

Well, when the credit-card bill shows up at the end of the month, needless to say, her husband is not a happy camper. There are a whole spectrum of ways in which he might react to the situation, but one thing is certain: he is not happy about it. His wife has directly disobeyed his known wishes. She has been devious in trying to cover up the deal. Furthermore, she has further exacerbated their already strained finances. In short, she has not done right by her husband.

Conversely, if I know my wife appreciates my picking up after myself and taking a little of the housework load from her, I routinely do so. Then I have done right by her. She comes up and gives me a kiss and says, "Thank you, Honey." By doing right by her and for her, I have made her happy and thereby added happiness to our relationship.

Suppose my wife knows I like to eat breakfast before I go out the door in the morning. She knows I like my egg turned just a certain way. Therefore, she gets up earlier than she would have otherwise, makes breakfast and turns the egg just the way I like it. On my way out the door, I give her a kiss and say, "Thank you, Honey. I love you." She got out of bed to do right by her husband. As a result, I was happy with her.

Incidentally, in part what motivated her to do right was *agape* love. Righteousness and *agape* love are closely related.

RIGHTEOUSNESS PRECEDES HAPPINESS

Have you noticed that there is a correlation between doing what is right by another and the degree of happiness we enjoy? Here is the reason: the work of righteousness is peace (Isa. 32:17). When I do right by my spouse (or anyone else for that matter), we will have some degree of peace.

Peace is the prerequisite of happiness. You will never be happy in general, much less happy with some individual, if you are not at peace. Peace is the absolute foundation upon which happiness is built.

The Declaration of Independence of this country speaks of the pursuit of happiness. Many people are running around pursuing happiness but never catching it. Happiness for them is like the proverbial pot of gold at the end of the rainbow. They are in continual pursuit of it, but they never seem to find it because they don't have peace in their lives. A major reason they don't have peace is that they have never allowed righteousness to take root. When individuals do unrighteously, even in seemingly little things: (a) they are not at peace with themselves because of the prick of conscience; (b) to some degree, they are not at peace with God; (c) if the deed in question has any relation to someone else, they are not at peace with that person. As a result, they are not genuinely happy.

Unrighteousness to any degree will unravel the potential

for happiness in our lives and often in the lives of those around us. Conversely, as we do what is right in any given situation, (a) there is a clear conscience—hence, peace of heart; (b) if others are involved, there will be peace among us; (c) we will be at peace with God. Righteousness precedes peace of heart and peace with others. It is the prerequisite of happiness.

Therefore, if I would be happy in my marriage relationship, it is incumbent upon me to do right by my spouse. Notice the chart below:

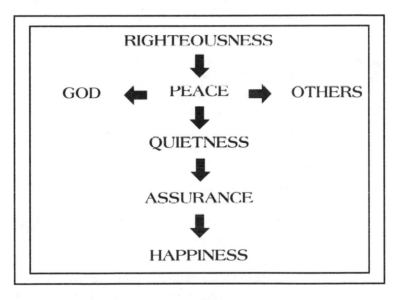

James 3:18 says, "And the fruit of righteousness is sown in peace of them that make peace." The result of doing right by or to another will be peace, and peace is the forerunner of happiness. Do you want happiness in your marriage? Do right by, to and for your mate. First will come a peaceful rapport with each other, and this will develop into happiness between you.

Over the years I have sought to apply the principle of

righteousness to real-life situations. I have concluded that many people don't think about whether a thing is right or not *before* they do it or leave it undone. It is far easier to observe *after* an act that it was or was not right than it is to think about it ahead of time. However, it is incumbent upon us to consider what is right *before* we do or say something.

The following are several areas of practical righteousness which pertain to doing right by our spouses:

PRACTICAL AREAS OF RIGHTEOUS-NESS IN A MARRIAGE

1. **We should do right in our attitudes toward our spouses.** Attitudes are quite abstract. They are difficult to define; nevertheless, they are very real. Though we at times cannot precisely articulate our own attitudes, they are there. We might not be able accurately to describe the attitudes of our spouses, but we surely can detect them. When our attitudes are right toward our spouses, we lay the foundation for peace and happiness.

An attitude of genuine respect for the feelings and concerns of one's spouse is right. When a spouse has an attitude of "I really don't care what you think," trouble is lurking ahead. There surely won't be much peace or happiness between each other.

In a coming chapter, we will develop the principle of submission by the wife toward her husband. However, for our purposes here, let me say, **submission is primarily an attitude.** I have observed wives who have the attitude, "Well, I'll do what you say, but on the inside I'll rebel." That is, among other things, not a right attitude. There will not be a great degree of happiness in such a relationship for either the husband or the wife.

I have watched husbands who have the attitude, "What

I do really isn't any of her business." Whether they get away with such an attitude is beside the point: there will not be much peace or happiness in such a relationship. Such an attitude just is not right. Knowing that peace and happiness follow righteousness is quite simple, isn't it?

Right attitudes in a marriage are built upon courtesy and mutual respect for each other. Again we come very close to the principle of *agape* love. When we love someone in an *agape* fashion, we will do what is right by that person, particularly in our attitudes. Love becomes the motive for doing right by our spouses.

2. **We should do right in the way we communicate to our spouses.** Let's face it: A smart mouth is never right. A disparaging mouth is not right. A foul mouth is never right. A nagging spirit is not right. A critical tongue is not right. Sarcastic lips are not right. Any problems existing in a given marriage are often exacerbated by the sharp tongue of one or the other.

Remember, kindness of word is right. Courtesy in conversation is right. Respect for the other in discussion is right. Speaking the truth in love is right. Inserting the dagger of our tongue and then twisting it is not right. It is right to compliment. It is right to say, "I love you." It is right to say, "I was wrong. I am sorry. Will you please forgive me." It is right to say "sweet nothings."

I have known couples who take some sort of perverse pleasure in always bantering with each other, using little put-downs and slams. Though that might be cute for awhile, sooner or later the little barbs and digs of sarcasm begin to pierce.

You will be much better served to follow the simple principle of always doing right verbally. Learn to develop the habit of analyzing what is about to cross the threshold of your lips with the little test, "Is it right?" Woe be to you if you "cop out" by telling yourself, "I know it's not right, but I am going to say it anyway." The loser will be you. If you sow the seeds of unrighteousness with your spouse, it will only engender discord. Guess who will be at least one of the unhappy people in your marriage. Do right in your communication with your spouse.

3. Do right by your spouse in eliminating extra work for him or her. Husbands usually are the guilty parties here. We become inconsiderate of our wives and all the work they do for us around the house. Consider who is going to pick up your pajamas if you don't. Woe be to you if you have the attitude, "Well, that's her job." The greater portion of the housework will fall to the wife, even if she works out of the home. Be considerate of her and do right by her in helping her in any way you can.

Whether it is picking up after yourself in the bathroom or picking up the newspapers strewn about the living room, consider that it is right to help your wife. It is right to help her with the children. It is right to help her with the dishes. It is right to help her in cleaning. Maybe she will not insist on such; but if the opportunity arises, it is right to be considerate and helpful.

It is right to put your dirty clothes in the hamper. It is right to hang up your coat. It is right to take off your shoes if they are dirty. It is right to help clean up after the children when they spill something.

Each home will establish its own guidelines for household chores. I am not suggesting any sort of role reversal here. What I am suggesting is that you do right by your spouse in helping him or her and eliminating extra hassle. Doing right by your spouse in this area comes back to the greater principle of giving of yourself for your mate. That is *agape* love.

When my wife went to work outside the home, I felt it

was my duty to help her more in household chores. She did not demand it. There was no sense of feminist liberation and role reversal. Rather, I loved her and wanted to help her and in so doing to do right by her.

Therefore, from time to time I will do the dishes for her. It is not because she has demanded that I be equal in sharing household chores. It is because I want to do right by her because I love her. I want to help relieve some of her load. At times I may make our bed in the morning as she is rushing to get ready. On other occasions, I will pick up around the house for her, especially if I know someone is coming over. My motive is to help her and eliminate extra work for her. I seek to do right by her because I love her.

I can't speak for her, but I think she has appreciated it. There is a peaceful rapport between us, and we are happy together. Doing right by and for each other has been a major part of the infrastructure of having a marriage which is heaven on earth.

4. **Do right by your spouse in being considerate of him or her.** Realize your spouse may be crabby because he or she is under pressure at work. Realize your spouse may be grumpy because he or she is not feeling great. Rise above just thinking about yourself and your feelings. Realize your spouse may not be all that he or she should be because there are problems unrelated to you that have his or her mind preoccupied. It is right to be thoughtful and considerate.

Be considerate in buying little gifts and tokens of appreciation. It is right to do so. Be considerate in letting him or her get extra sleep when it is needed. Be considerate in courteously participating in family functions with your in-laws, even though such events may not be your idea of a good time. It is right to be considerate of your spouse.

5. **Do right by your spouse in how your money is handled.** We will take the entire next chapter to discuss the matter of money and marriage, but here suffice it to say that this is a crucial point. I have been aware of spouses who sneak around behind the backs of their husbands or wives and buy things and then conceal them. That is devious, and it certainly isn't right. Whether it is sneaking money from your husband's billfold while he is asleep or buying that fishing or hunting gear without your wife's knowledge, it is not right.

In other cases, deviousness is not the issue. For some, bickering over the checkbook or credit card becomes a point of contention. Usually self-focused living is at the core of debate. Whether it is a wife whining about why she can't buy things for the house or a husband pouting about why his wife opposes his latest project, the problem is self-focused. It simply is not right! Immaturity is involved. *Agape* love is cast aside. None of these falls within the parameters of doing what is right.

Be completely open and honest with your spouse in all financial dealings. As a rule of thumb, set his or her interests ahead of your own. All things being equal (budget, family needs, checkbook balance, for example), be willing to bend as your spouse desires to purchase something.

6. **Do right by your spouse in how time is spent.** This concept is very similar to the preceding. Consider the wife who stays at home and takes care of the children, takes care of the house, takes care of the laundry, and takes care of her husband. She is busy, but she longs for the fellowship of her husband.

Then he gets off work and after gobbling down a quick supper, heads out the door to do things with his buddies. She sits home alone all evening. In modern life there are enough extraneous functions to eat up our "free" time. They are activities such as church, school and political functions, and community events. To ignore one's spouse and continually run after personal interests is just not right, nor is it considerate.

I direct this more toward husbands, because they usually

are guiltier at this point. There may be nothing wrong with the after-work softball team, but be very careful of your time for your wife's sake. Do right by her. There is nothing wrong with fishing or hunting per se, but be careful that you do not rob from your spouse time which is rightfully hers. We come right back to the idea of being thoughtful, being mature—back to *agape* love.

7. Do right by your spouse in how you vent your emotions. The truth is, venting negative emotions frequently is not right. It is not right to lose your temper. It is not right to cry as a device to get your way. It is not right to pout. It is not right to disinter old troubles and hash them out again. It is not right to vent ugliness. Righteousness of character will preclude a multitude of problems which take peace and happiness out of a marriage.

8. Do right by your spouse in being careful of his or her things. This is a subset of being considerate, which is a function of doing right. Husbands will carelessly track in dirt on their wives' clean floors. They will bring a gun or some auto part into the house to clean it and in so doing will foul up the kitchen. In cleaning out closets wives throw out all the junk accumulated there. In so doing, they discard some of their husbands' little treasures. I have known wives to allow the kids to play with their fathers' golf clubs or fishing gear and mess them all up. Doing right by your spouse is simply being considerate of him and his things.

9. Do right by your spouse in fidelity. A married person's flirting with someone else simply is not right. Letting your eyes follow someone else is not right. Being alone with a person of the opposite sex, if not wrong, can often be perilous. Nothing may ever happen, but it does no good for your spouse and your relationship.

After all is said and done, the simple fact is, infidelity is not right! Not only is adultery a breach of *agape* love, it simply is not right. If we would precede any improper thought or flirtation with the simple question, "Is it right?" most such sin would be precluded. When righteousness as a practical principle has been woven into the warp and woof of the fabric of our character, it will serve as a strong deterrent against infidelity. Just do what is right.

Jesus spoke about looking on a woman to lust after her as having committed adultery in the heart. (Incidentally, the Bible elsewhere teaches that what we think in our hearts is the forerunner of what we do.) There are two important principles here: First, men need to discipline their eyes and minds to look at what is right. In this day of immodesty and provocative dress, it is very easy for an immodestly dressed woman to catch the eye of a Christian man. Righteousness says not to gaze upon her. You may not be able to prevent seeing her in the first place, but you don't have to keep looking. This is exactly what got David into trouble with Bathsheba.

Likewise, Christian women need to be careful about how they dress. The Apostle Paul enjoined godly women to dress in modest attire (I Tim. 2:9). There never is any justification for adultery; but unfortunately, in more than one case, the man has been enticed by a woman who dressed in a way which was not altogether right.

In the matter of being faithful to your spouse, just remember the simple admonition, "Do what is right!" That pretty much sums it up.

In conclusion, remember that righteousness is a significant part of the infrastructure of your marriage. Doing right is often not much noticed; leaving it undone is obvious. Then it becomes a bone of contention. Remember that righteousness is the precursor of peace, which is the prerequisite for happiness. These are absolutely necessary ingredients to a marriage which is heaven on earth.

7.

FAMILY FINANCES

In this the final chapter of this section, we return to the idea of infrastructure. The infrastructure of a city is largely unseen and is ignored by most of the city's population. Most people think very little about the water distribution system. They think little of gas mains and, of all things, sanitary sewers. Very few people concern themselves with the understructure of bridges. We take those things for granted, and as long as they work, we never give them a thought.

But one night the water main serving your neighborhood breaks. You awaken to no water, and at once your life is in chaos. There is no water to drink nor with which to bathe, and you can't flush the toilets. Then on your way to work, you find the arterial street leading from Point A to Point B is washed out by the water main break. Abruptly, the infrastructure of your city has become very real to you. It is only when the sewer is plugged, the bridge is out, or the gas main is broken that we concern ourselves with such things as common as infrastructure.

In the preceding chapter we dealt with the principle of righteousness and how it is a part of the infrastructure of a happy marriage. Here we will delve into an even more practical matter which certainly is a part of the infrastructure of our marriages. That is family finances.

Family finances, or the way we handle our money, is a substantial part of the infrastructure of a marriage. When everything is going okay in this department, we don't think much about it. When times are good and the money is flowing in faster than it is flowing out, there are not many problems. But sooner or later (usually sooner) the money will stop flowing in faster than it flows out. Unless there are careful safeguards and practices in place, the handling of money can become a major source of contention and trouble in a marriage relationship.

As most marriage counselors know, family finances are the number one cause for marriage trouble and divorce. I think about the many marriage counseling sessions I have had. A majority have in some way involved money problems.

In the New Testament, Jesus taught more about money than He taught about Heaven and how to get there.

When money begins to be a problem in a marriage, it often brings out the worst in people. It exacerbates other problems and heightens the weaknesses in the marriage. The truth is, few people have no money worries. Money and family finances get right down to where we live. Though we usually do not like to admit it, the status of our financial affairs is a thermometer which considerably measures the relative success of our lives. It definitely will affect a marriage, especially if things in this area are not going well.

FIVE FINANCIAL PROBLEM AREAS

Let us look at five financial problem areas which crop up in many marriages. These things by themselves may not put a marriage at risk (though often they do). However, at the least, these five problem areas can surely sour a marriage relationship. In contrast, good family financial practices can be a significant building block in the foundation of a marriage which is heavenly.

1. **Pressure from bills.** Many of us have been where there is more month than money. Bills show up in the mailbox in inverse proportion to the balance in the checking account. A bill collector calls and adds tension to our nerves and points to our blood pressure. An annual insurance bill we always forget shows up. Medical bills we had not counted on arrive. The utility company calls and threatens to shut off the water. The children bring home a list of school materials that have to be purchased. The furnace quits. The transmission on the car has to be rebuilt. The credit card bill arrives. The dog has to have surgery. The property tax is delinquent. And April 15 is looming—the IRS accounting deadline. On top of that, your spouse wants to spend money for his or her favorite pursuit.

As tension builds, gloom and despair set in. People become crabby toward their spouses. When bills arrive, there is finger-pointing about why a certain thing was purchased. "Why didn't we talk about this first? What gave you the right to spend that? How come you only think about yourself? You are just selfish! Why are you spending all our money?" One can imagine the rest of the impending fights.

The way we handle our money has the potential to build tranquillity in a home. It also can be the catalyst for ugly arguing, bitterness, frustration and incessant fighting.

I think of a stereotypical couple. Jim's work from year to year was not predictable. Forces of international econometrics controlled the industry in which he worked. Some years he had a flood of overtime. Other years were a drought, with numerous layoffs.

So Sue, his wife, worked part-time to help stabilize family finances. When times were good and the money was rolling in, things went smoothly; but when times slowed down, invariably trouble erupted in the marriage. Though the income slowed, the spending continued unabated. Bills began to pile up. Bill collectors harassed, and utility companies threatened to turn off supplies. Jim and Sue quit tithing, rationalizing that they couldn't afford to do it.

At home, Jim and Sue fought over why the bills were so

high. She pointed her finger at him and accused him of running up bills on things for his boat. He pointed his finger at her and accused her of running up long-distance phone bills by calling her parents.

The acrimony spilled over into other parts of their marriage. The closeness of their fellowship and friendship became strained. They became irritable and bickered over any little thing.

Because of the friction at home, Jim tried to find ways to stay away from home. He bowled more, played on a softball team, and found ways to occupy his time away from home. All of the potential for other marriage trouble was lurking close by.

What was the root of all of this discord? The way Jim and Sue handled their finances.

From my experience it seems that pressure from bills stems from three sources: **one is uncontrolled spending.** Some people spend money like there is no tomorrow.

Let's look at another stereotypical situation. Linda had come from a home where there was never any lack. Both her parents had good-paying positions. Her parents' home was comfortable, and they tasted a bit of the good life.

Linda's young husband, Chuck, had grown up during good years for his parents. The company for which his dad had worked prospered, and the family shared in its prosperity. When Chuck and Linda were married, their earning power was only a fraction of their parents'. Yet they wanted to maintain the lifestyle to which they were accustomed in their upbringing.

As children came, Linda quit working to stay home with them. Chuck and she had already bought a new home. Furthermore, they had bought all new furniture, on credit of course. The neighborhood they lived in was moderately nice—not exclusive, but not shabby. Linda buzzed around in a used but fairly late-model sedan. Chuck had bought a new pickup truck and spread out the payments for five years. By the time the truck was three and one-half years old, it needed major repairs. He still owed eighteen months' worth of payments on it.

A recession set in. Chuck's income took a dip. Up to this point, they had been "making it" financially, though barely; but then things got tough. They fell behind in the mortgage payments. Each month as the routine bills of life showed up, there was frustration as they juggled their reduced resources to pacify the loudest bill collector.

Of course, the pressure backed up into their marriage relationship like a backed-up sewer. The problem was their spending. They had foolishly overspent their ability to pay.

A brief study of American history will reveal that the national economy is predictably cyclical. That is, there are periods of prosperity that sooner or later are followed by periods of recession and, occasionally, depression. The cycle is almost like a sine wave that routinely goes up and down. Economists know the cycle. They just cannot accurately predict when or to what degree each period on the cycle will take place.

Unfortunately, many young couples borrow and spend during years of prosperity, never contemplating the fact that there will come times of recession. Moreover, local and regional economies fluctuate. Regions and communities that were hotbeds of prosperity a decade or a generation ago become depressed, and other areas start booming.

I grew up in a community which didn't really feel the effects of a national recession for about twenty years. People in that community borrowed and spent like there was no tomorrow. Then one day economic forces caught up with that community, and the bottom fell out. It took almost a decade for it to recover. Meanwhile, unemployment skyrocketed, and homes by the hundreds were foreclosed. Family after family went through deep crisis. Sadly, many a marriage took a beating.

The point of this discussion of the economic cycle is that couples who foolishly borrow and spend are setting themselves up for a crisis. It will vary in degree, depending upon circumstances, but one can just about count on the fact that good times will be followed by leaner times.

Another related area of trouble is **credit card spending.** Twenty years ago, general credit cards—such as MasterCard and Visa, issued by banks—were not well known. Today, they are ubiquitous. There is not a month, and sometimes not a week, when we do not receive advertisements by mail or phone seeking to induce us to subscribe to some slick credit card offer.

When my daughters graduated from high school, they were promptly solicited to subscribe to somebody's credit card.

Credit cards, per se, are not wrong; but for some, they are a disaster waiting to happen. Unfortunately, credit card mania has disastrous consequences in some marriages. One would think people would realize, when purchasing with credit cards, that they are eventually going to have to "pay the piper." (Inevitably, it is with outrageous interest.) Yet some young couples go out and begin racking up credit card bills like they are going out of style. However, for credit card users, tomorrow does come. Usually it's at the end of the month.

To make matters worse, most credit card companies require only a minimum payment each month, and this extends the user's addiction. One day unforeseen circumstances are brought to bear, and the credit card bills cannot be paid, not even the minimums. Then the collection agencies begin calling, and other nasty pressures begin to worm their way into the marriage. Frustration, pressure, friction and much unhappiness are the inevitable result.

The moral of this story is, credit cards ought to be used only for unforeseen emergencies or for convenience. As this chapter is being written, I have unfortunately incurred a major, unexpected repair bill on my car. The payment of the bill was placed on a credit card. During the next month I will be moving money from a savings account to pay that bill because there is not enough cash on hand to meet the need. Some of it may have to be paid in installments, but it was essentially an emergency situation in which I had no choice.

I define *convenience use* of a credit card as purchasing most anything, often routine things such as gasoline, with the firm knowledge that the bill will be paid *in full* when it arrives later in the month. The credit card thereby becomes a convenience in that one must not always carry enough cash in his pocket to buy routine necessities.

Carrying a balance on a credit card for discretionary spending will likely bring duress to family finances. It is also unwise. Even when the much-touted annual percentage rates are lowered a bit, there is still the potential to pay from nine to eighteen percent interest. Any amount of financial acumen will determine the foolish nature of paying that kind of interest, but that is how banks make much of their money.

Still another area bringing financial pressure is **a lack of tithing which brings a lack of God's blessing.** The Bible is quite clear that God has entrusted His people with the tithe and has commanded that we honor Him with it. When Christians withhold the tithe, they place themselves in a place where God cannot and will not bless them, particularly financially.

Malachi 3:8–10 is a unique dialogue between God and His people through the Prophet Malachi. Since God knew their hearts, He knew the response of His people as He spoke through the prophet. God rhetorically asked the question, "Will a man rob God?"

Because God knew their hearts, we can read their response: "Wherein have we robbed thee?"

God's answer was simple: "In tithes and offerings."

In verse 9, God went on to remind them, "Ye are cursed with a curse: for ye have robbed me." The fact is, Israel was in a jam economically. They made their living largely from agricultural products. Because they had not only disobeyed God by not tithing but they had also, in effect, embezzled from Him, God had removed His blessing from their crops and had placed a curse upon them. Their farms and gardens were overrun with devouring insects. There was drought. Furthermore, there were high winds and early frosts, damaging any remaining crops. God said, "Ye are cursed with a curse."

His rejoinder to Israel was simple: "Bring ye all the tithes into the storehouse, that there may be meat in mine house, and prove me now herewith, saith the LORD of hosts, if I will not open you the windows of heaven, and pour you out a blessing, that there shall not be room enough to receive it." God promised His people this: If they would honor and obey Him by bringing their tithes to the storehouse, He would open the windows of Heaven and bless them. The drought would end. God would drive the clouds of insects from their fields, and He would withhold damaging weather from their crops.

There is a double application here: First, when a Christian faithfully tithes, he places himself where God can bless his personal finances. "And all the tithe of the land...is the LORD'S: it is holy unto the LORD" (Lev. 27:30). The tithe is the Lord's, whether we return it to Him or not. It is His, and He has entrusted it to us. When we give it back to Him, we have honored Him by obeying Him. The simple fact is, God has promised to bless those who so obey and trust Him (Mal. 3:10).

On the other hand, when a Christian withholds the tithe, he is actually embezzling what God has entrusted to him. How can we expect God to bless us when we systematically embezzle from Him? He knows it, and He in turn will remove His blessing from our affairs and perhaps even curse those affairs.

What does that have to do with marriage and family finances? Very simply, people who won't tithe are likely to have financial pressure in their homes. God's blessing is not on them; and they, in all likelihood, are afflicted by a curse of God on their affairs.

There are many excuses people make for not tithing. People complain that they can't afford to tithe. The truth is that we can't afford *not* to tithe. People are often in a financial "pickle," in part, for not tithing. By withholding the tithe, they move themselves from God's blessing to His curse on their financial affairs.

Others seek to excuse themselves from tithing because they are in a low-income bracket. God never set a starting point for tithing. It is equilateral, across the board. Ten percent for a low-income person is the same proportion as ten percent for an affluent person.

When I was five years old, my father taught me to tithe. I began by giving back to God a nickel of my fifty-cent allowance each week. When I became a paperboy, my tithe was a dollar of my ten-dollar weekly profit. I know a person whose annual income is two hundred thousand dollars. His excuse for not tithing is that he cannot afford it. "Why, that is twenty thousand dollars a year! I can't afford *that!*" Ten percent is ten percent.

We zero in on the home and family financial troubles. As a pastor, I do not check the church records to see who gave what. I have always considered that between an individual and the Lord. However, I often know who tithes and who doesn't because people talk. People who tithe often give testimony of it and how the Lord blesses them in return. People who don't tithe often grumble that the church always begs for money. They tell others they don't tithe, and sooner or later the pastor knows.

I think of a stereotypical situation from my years of observation. George and Sally didn't tithe. They figured that placing their children in the Christian school compensated for tithing. Nevertheless, they always had enough money for recreational and entertainment pursuits. They claimed they just couldn't afford to tithe. Besides, they said, the church could get along without their help.

George got laid off from his job. Sally went to work trying to supplement his unemployment check. During that time, the furnace went out, and their car threw a rod. One of their children wound up with medical bills when their health insurance had run out. Because Sally was working, the house was a mess. George was not much inclined to do laundry or wash dishes, and things started to pile up.

Sally would come home, and invariably there would be fighting over the fact that George wouldn't do anything to help around the house. Then the fighting turned to who spent what, when and why. Their family life became one big frazzle. There were pressures and problems in their home in part because they refused to honor the Lord in tithing.

Consider the case of John and Alice. Alice believed that they ought to tithe, but John didn't want to. He made up excuses about its being legalistic and said they couldn't afford to do it. Well, Alice tithed anyway of the pay from her part-time job, but John wouldn't tithe of his paycheck.

It seemed like something was always going wrong. The transmission on John's van went out, and it cost him a thousand dollars to fix it. He had to have dental work done, and it ran into hundreds of dollars. The refrigerator quit and had to be replaced. The roof had to be fixed after a storm blew a tree onto it. Their insurance wouldn't cover it because of some quirky clause. Then at work John was bumped into a lower-paying position. "Why, there is no way I can tithe. Look at all the financial problems I've got!"

John was cursed with a curse. Why? Because he was intentionally and regularly robbing God.

Folks, you will never get out from behind the eight ball financially until you faithfully tithe. The financial pressures in your home that result from not tithing are going to take the "honey" out of your honeymoon. You cannot gyp God and prosper or be happy for long.

2. **Friction over priorities.** We come back to the basic problem of selfishness, which is immaturity. Friction from wrong priorities reveals a lack of *agape* love and a lack of righteousness. Immature couples want certain things because they want them. Then they fight about them.

Rick and Cheri were both spoiled. Both were immature adults. Rick loved out-of-door activities. He loved to be with the guys. He liked to hunt, and he liked to fish. He liked sports. He had a fairly good job and a decent part-time job he fit in as he liked. He brought home a good income. For a young couple, they had no immediate financial pressures.

Therefore, Rick bought a nice new pickup truck with the fancy molded running boards, mag-type wheels, chrome roll bars and a fancy paint job. Cheri complained bitterly about his spending so much money. As far as she was concerned, their car worked okay.

Rick then decided to get an all-terrain vehicle to play with. He said it would help him when he went hunting. They had a big fight over that.

Then Rick invested a significant amount of cash in a new hunting gun. Cheri deeply resented that. She wanted to put new carpet in the living room. Rick prevailed. Then Rick decided to get a used fishing boat. Then it needed a new and larger motor.

Meanwhile, Cheri wanted to do other redecorating of the house, but Rick spent all of their discretionary income on *his* things. One day he brought home an expensive, pedigreed hunting dog. He had never talked to her about it; he just showed up with the puppy. That of course meant a doghouse and a kennel needed to be built. Because there were veterinary bills, Cheri's projects were sidetracked.

When they came in for marriage counseling, Rick couldn't understand why his wife was being such a witch. "All she ever does is yell at me and nag me." Their marriage was just about the opposite of heaven on earth. Though they did not have financial troubles from pressure of unpaid bills, Rick's selfish spending caused endless friction. Eventually they divorced.

3. **Distrust caused by deviousness.** Some people think that they can somehow hide things from their spouses and live happily ever after.

Jan was a mall denizen. She loved to check out the area shopping malls. She didn't particularly want to *buy* things; she just liked to *shop*. However, when she went shopping, she often found things she liked. She took out a credit card in her own name and never told her husband, Bob. From her part-time job, she had a small income. She was usually home when the mailman came, so she would intercept the mail and pull out her own credit card bill before her husband saw the mail.

Bob saw things around the house that seemed new, but he never paid much attention to them. When he asked about them, Jan would say, "Oh, my mother gave that to me," or, "I found that at a garage sale."

One day, however, Bob happened to be home when the mailman came, and he got to the mail before Jan did. He said, "What's this credit card bill? We don't have a credit card with this store." He opened it up and saw the various purchases Jan had made over the last month and the balance which was carried over. He blew his top. He hollered, "Why didn't you talk to me about this? All you would have had to do was ask. I don't care if you want to buy stuff. How come you have to sneak around behind my back and hide things from me?"

That day a major pillar in Bob and Jan's marriage had been toppled—his trust of her. She had proven herself devious and deceptive. She had lied to him. He wondered how much more she was hiding. Since she would cheat on finances, would she cheat on him otherwise?

Their marriage went from average to rocky. Thereafter, every time they fought he would bring up the matter of her sneakiness, and she would throw back at him, "Why won't you ever forgive or forget?" Then she would lament, "You don't trust me!" Though the couple stayed together, that incident haunted them for years to come. Their relationship was not exactly heaven on earth.

An analogy could easily be developed of husbands who bought things they didn't want their wives to see and hid them in garages or sheds. Sooner or later, the matters surfaced, and then all sorts of troubles erupted.

Being devious can unravel a major strand holding a marriage together. That strand is trust. Once it is broken, it is hard to mend.

4. Goals based on financial ambition. The Apostle Paul wrote:

"But they that will be rich fall into temptation and a snare, and into many foolish and hurtful lusts, which drown men in destruction

and perdition. For the love of money is the root of all evil: which while some coveted after, they have erred from the faith, and pierced themselves through with many sorrows."—I Tim. 6:9,10.

I have seen several couples get into marriage trouble because financial goals caused false expectations. Others have allowed the drive to succeed financially to be disruptive to their marriages.

In the wedding ceremony, often the little phrase "for better or for worse" is used. Unfortunately, some couples "fall into temptation and a snare" over the love of money, and they 'pierce themselves through with many sorrows.'

Don and Fran were in business for themselves. Fran saw Don as a ticket to advancement in life. As the business developed and prospered, things went all right. They at times fought and argued, but since things were progressing, they stayed on course.

They built a new home in an upscale neighborhood. Their name was displayed all over town in their advertising. Though the cash flow of their business was oftentimes unpredictable, to the community they were examples of success and prosperity.

Then business took a nose dive. Bills mounted. Pressures built. Finally, in despair, they went out of business. They had to sell their new home, and no longer were they the picture of success in town. Rather, they were perceived as having lost it.

Don just "kept on keeping on." He tried to pick up the pieces and go on from there. But Fran had had enough. She figured Don was a loser, and their marriage began to go on the rocks.

We could say this situation evidenced a lack of genuine *agape* love and that it was characterized by emotional and spiritual immaturity. Indeed, that would be a fair analysis.

But the trip wire which set off their troubles was an unhealthy attitude toward money. In particular, Fran's love of prosperity and success "pierced" their marriage "through with many sorrows."

With Larry and Ann, the scenario was different. Still an improper perspective on money almost destroyed their marriage. Larry had a good job. He also had an intense desire to advance financially. Therefore, he always had a second and sometimes a third job. It was not so much that he was a workaholic, but rather that he had one goal in mind, and that was to get ahead. All he did was work. He spent prudently and was even tightfisted. Every dollar which was not absolutely needed for household expense was invested for additional gain.

At first, Ann was proud they were making headway financially; but after awhile, it became evident Larry had little time for her or the children. His goal was almost a god to him. They spent little time together. They did not have much time to talk. Though Ann complained about their deteriorating fellowship, Larry brushed her off. His sidelines and investments were starting to pick up steam. He got so busy making money he did not even notice his wife's drifting away.

By the time they came for marriage counseling, it was almost too late. Larry's financial ambition had dug a gulf between him and his wife.

5. **Lost confidence from mismanagement.** Shelly and Mark were a young couple who were a stereotype of another kind of problem involving money and marriage. Shelly adored Mark. She almost worshiped the ground on which he walked. Their marriage maintained the "honey" in the honeymoon long after they were married.

Mark felt strongly that the husband was to be the head

of the house, and that especially meant handling the money. The pride of his leadership in the home bordered on his being stubborn and a bullhead. He was the head of the house, and Shelly accepted it.

Unfortunately, Mark was a poor manager. He kept poor records and was an impulse buyer. At times he forgot to record checks in the checkbook register. That in turn caused some checks to bounce because of insufficient funds. He would excuse it to his wife by blaming the bank for the mistake.

He slipped into the bad habit of credit card spending. Shelly never saw the credit card statements nor the bank statements. Mark took care of those. Eventually, all Mark could manage were the minimum credit card payments each month. Though he was beginning to be aware of impending trouble, Shelly knew nothing about it. Mark was too proud to tell her about it. As his mismanagement continued, he couldn't even make the minimum monthly payments. Other bills were more pressing, so he paid them.

Well, one day Shelly received a phone call from a collection agency which rudely and ominously informed her if they didn't pay up, dire things were going to happen to them. Shelly was dumbfounded. She had trusted Mark to take care of their finances. Now she sensed something was terribly wrong. Furthermore, she deeply resented the fact Mark had hid these problems from her.

When he came home, things erupted. Not only was the blossom off the rose of their marriage, but also she had lost confidence in her husband. By mismanaging family finances and covering up the impending crisis, Mark had shattered a foundational block of their marriage. This had long-term consequences.

* * *

These various areas of financial troubles can certainly

cause a marriage to be anything but heaven on earth. At the worst, they can break a marriage apart.

Let us consider five bits of financial advice which can keep the financial infrastructure of a marriage stable and strong.

FIVE BITS OF ADVICE

These five points are of practical help as far as finances and marriage are concerned. They are not intended to be a section on how to succeed financially or how to make good investments. These concern the relationship of finances to marriage.

1. **Stop credit purchases!** There are probably only two things which should be purchased on credit: one is a home; the other is a vehicle. The latter is really a very poor transaction in the greater perspective of finances. However, most people can't obtain a reliable vehicle, particularly early in life, without some sort of financing. Apart from these, one should not buy on credit, period.

If you maintain credit cards, use them only for emergencies or as convenience items. As described earlier, convenience use of a credit card is purchasing routine items and then paying the bill *in full* at the end of the month. If you cannot discipline yourself to refrain from impulse buying, it is best not to carry a credit card.

Ignore all the high-power promotional hype, like "zero down and no payments for ninety days." Do not buy on credit! If you want something, save for it. That takes discipline and self-control. You will remove financial pressures from your marriage by eliminating bills and hassles over them. You also will be on the road to better financial health.

By buying on credit, you are probably going to pay at least eighteen percent interest. When you factor in the interest that will accrue from letting cash build up for a purchase, you probably will have a savings difference of over twenty percent. That is significant. Halt all credit purchasing of any kind, with the two exceptions mentioned above.

2. Tithe. As described above, it is a spiritual matter of obeying God and trusting Him to provide. It also is a means of realizing God's blessing on your affairs. Tithing will not make you rich, but tithing will put God's blessing on you and your finances. Tithing will thus stabilize your financial life. Moreover, regular tithing requires financial discipline in keeping track of income and outgo. That in itself can be of great benefit.

My wife and I have always sought to put the Lord first in money matters. We have done this not only by returning to God a minimum of the tithe, but by making our giving to the Lord the first priority of our budget. In other words, our giving to the Lord of the tithe (and offerings over and above) takes precedence over all spending.

"Honour the LORD with thy substance, and with the firstfruits of all thine increase: So shall thy barns be filled with plenty."— Prov. 3:9,10.

Honoring the Lord with your giving will stabilize your financial setup and will even concentrate God's blessing on your affairs. In so doing, you will eliminate many of the financial pressures which are harmful to marriage.

3. Throttle unnecessary spending. I am continually amazed as I watch people who I know are struggling financially. Most are victims of impulse spending. Not only is this a character weakness, but it also perpetuates financial distress.

Shortly, we will discuss having a working budget; but at this point, suffice it to say, impulse buying and a budget are opposites. Impulse spending will bring financial stress to your marriage by increasing bills and/or diminishing cash.

Stress will also come from your having to justify to your spouse why you bought a certain item.

Unless you are in excellent shape financially, avoid going out to eat. Some people, whose marriages are strained because of financial struggles, routinely eat out. There is nothing wrong with eating at a restaurant; but if you are on thin ice financially, it is unwise.

Mike and Vicki were struggling financially. The pressure of bills had backed up into their marriage, and they fought regularly over money, bills and how to juggle it all. Yet every week they took their entire family out to a local restaurant for a meal. It wasn't a top-dollar place, but it wasn't McDonald's either. If they had sat down and multiplied their weekly restaurant tab by fifty-two, they would have been amazed at what sizable bills they could have retired in a year's time.

Most people know they could eat at home for a fraction of the cost of a restaurant meal; but Vicki excused her family's practice by saying, "Well, I cook all the time. I deserve a break once a week." Maybe so; but when their family was at risk from financial pressures, they were only adding fuel to the fire.

Other families who are struggling to survive financially regularly order pizza from a quick-delivery pizza place. When some sort of fancy entertainment comes to town, they pay the inflated price for tickets. People who have trouble paying the utility bills are often the ones who keep the clothing stores in business.

There is also the endless buying of toys. Someone once said the only difference between a boy and a man is the price of the toys they buy. These things may not be wrong in themselves; however, when a marriage is under stress from financial pressure, unnecessary spending is foolish.

If you find your family finances in a bind, force yourself

onto an austere program of buying only absolute necessities and nothing else. In fact, that is a rather good philosophy anyway.

In contrast to the spendthrifts, some more prosperous and affluent people have always lived lives of financial restraint, limiting their buying and controlling their spending. That's how they got ahead. As an added bonus, they never faced the pressures and fighting which often accompany unnecessary spending.

4. **Save.** Most people don't save because they are too busy spending money "to the max" and then some. I once heard a financial advisor say many American families spend 110 percent of their annual income. Saving is prudent in preparing for retirement. It is also a safety net for times of unforeseen trouble. Savings can relieve pressure in your marriage when things go wrong. Though you hate to spend savings, doing so might offset a crisis in your family.

5. **Set up a working budget and live by it.** I have reserved perhaps the most important tip for last. On a practical level, a working budget can be the framework of carrying out the four preceding bits of advice. Without a working budget, your finances will be shaky. I say "working budget." Many people sit down and *propose* a budget but then put it in the kitchen junk drawer. They find it three years later when the drawer is so full it gets stuck. A working budget is a document that guides you on a monthly and even weekly basis.

Estimate what you spend on various items monthly. After you have done that, multiply the total by twelve to estimate your annual spending. You may find you are planning to spend more than your net income. Then begin to prune various items from your list until your projected spending equals your net income. Each month record against your monthly budget projection how much you have actually spent. You can then determine where you are financially and make adjustments to keep on an even keel.

If you set up a family budget properly and *live by it,* you can stabilize your finances and even prepare for unexpected eventualities.

Here are some practical pointers that can help make a budget work for you:

a. In setting up your budget, include *everything* you spend. Leave out nothing. Though you may lump some things together, put down *everything* on which your money is spent. Obvious things—such as mortgage or rent, groceries, utilities, debt reduction, all manner of insurance, gasoline and all other auto expenses, car payments, clothing and school expenses—need to be listed. Things not quite so obvious are your tithe, taxes, camp for the kids, eating out, entertainment, savings, pet expenses, vacation, Christmas expenses, gifts, medicine and even pocket change.

b. Discipline yourself to keep records. Most people don't keep a budget because they do not discipline themselves to do the necessary record-keeping. It is tedious, but it can help stabilize your family finances.

There are ready-made forms at stationery and office supply stores which can help you in doing a budget, or you can make up your own record system just as well. There are excellent family finance computer programs which make such record-keeping very easy. **However you do it, do it!**

Keep accurate records of your income, not only for tax purposes, but also so that you know exactly how much is really coming in. More tedious is keeping a record of everything you spend.

In our home, we have tried to make a paper trail of everything we spend. Therefore, we try to do the vast majority of our transactions by either check or a check/debit card. By doing business in this fashion, it is relatively easy to keep track of where our money goes. At the end of the month, it is fairly easy to plug that information into our budget system.

c. **Appoint one person to be the main comptroller and treasurer of the family.** One person always needs to be on top of family finances. If the husband is good at record-keeping, perhaps he should be the one. Sometimes the wife is more adept and skilled at so doing. One person may have more time than the other to take care of the records. One person should be the comptroller in the sense of always knowing what the balances and budget are. This also makes a good forum for communication about family finances and purchases. From not only a monetary but also a communication standpoint, always talk about spending and your financial situation.

d. **The key to it all is personal discipline.** More than anything else, the key to stabilizing family finances is *discipline*. Discipline is controlling the spending. Discipline is keeping records. Discipline is producing a monthly budget analysis. Discipline is forcing yourself to do what may be tedious and boring. Discipline is insisting that you do what *ought* to be done and not what you *feel* like doing. Discipline in the area of finances will solve almost all the problems detailed in this chapter.

e. **Program saving and tithing into your budget.** You will likely never tithe nor save much if you do not plan to do so. Make sure these things have high priority in your family budget.

Family finances may not seem exciting nor romantic; however, it is a part of the infrastructure of a marriage. Without a sound infrastructure, your marriage will have significant problems. Discipline yourself to do what you *ought* to do with your money, rather than what you *want* to do with it. It will make a profound difference. As you remove financial problems from your marriage, you will be removing a major source of marital discord.

SECTION III

SCRIPTURE PASSAGES REGARDING MARRIAGE

8.
AN EXPOSITION OF EPHESIANS 5:21–33

THE BRIDE OF CHRIST

One of the things with which the Epistle to the Ephesians deals is the unique relationship between Jesus Christ and the church. Throughout the New Testament, the church of Jesus Christ is described as the *bride* of Christ. Someday when Jesus Christ returns in the rapture, it will be to take His espoused bride unto Himself in the grandest wedding ceremony that has ever taken place. That wedding ceremony will be in Heaven. It is referred to as the marriage supper of the Lamb in Revelation 19:7–9. After the marriage, Christ will return with His bride to this earth for what some have likened to a one-thousand-year honeymoon, the millennial kingdom. The Epistle to the Ephesians has perhaps more references to the impending marriage between Jesus Christ and the church than any other part of the Bible.

From Ephesians 5 it is evident that the church of Jesus Christ is His wife-in-prospect. Moreover, it is clear that the institution of human marriage is parallel to and patterned after the relationship between Jesus Christ and the church. The chapter enlightens us about the relationship between Jesus Christ and the church, which is the *pattern* for the relationship between a husband and wife.

"Submitting yourselves one to another in the fear of God.

"Wives, submit yourselves unto your own husbands, as unto the Lord.

"For the husband is the head of the wife, even as Christ is the head of the church: and he is the saviour of the body.

"Therefore as the church is subject unto Christ, so let the wives be to their own husbands in every thing.

"Husbands, love your wives, even as Christ also loved the church, and gave himself for it;

"That he might sanctify and cleanse it with the washing of water by the word,

"That he might present it to himself a glorious church, not having spot, or wrinkle, or any such thing; but that it should be holy and without blemish.

"So ought men to love their wives as their own bodies. He that loveth his wife loveth himself.

"For no man ever yet hated his own flesh; but nourisheth and cherisheth it, even as the Lord the church:

"For we are members of his body, of his flesh, and of his bones.

"For this cause shall a man leave his father and mother, and shall be joined unto his wife, and they two shall be one flesh.

"This is a great mystery: but I speak concerning Christ and the church.

"Nevertheless let every one of you in particular so love his wife even as himself; and the wife see that she reverence her husband."—Eph. 5:21–33.

With obvious reference to Christ and the church, the passage sets forth basic principles of the relationship a husband and wife ought to have to each other.

A COOPERATIVE SPIRIT

Some might question whether verse 21 is a part of the direct teaching on marriage. However, it is indisputable that it is part of the immediate context. I am of the opinion it forms an important backdrop for the husband-wife relationship.

Here Paul says, "Submitting yourselves one to another in the fear of God." We shall see that God has ordained a unique relationship wherein the wife is submissive to her husband. By way of introduction, however, Paul touches upon a broader principle of married life. Both husband and wife ought to have a submissive *attitude* toward each other in decisions that do not challenge the husband's authority in the home. The idea is of a *cooperative* spirit between husband and wife.

We will see that the husband indeed is the ultimate head of the home as far as authority is concerned. In verse 21 that is not the issue. There are many day-to-day matters in which both husband and wife need to have a *cooperative* and submissive spirit.

For example, though the husband is the head of the marriage, it may not be wise for him to "pull rank" in every little decision. Perhaps his wife wishes to go to the mall, and he wants to go to the sporting goods store. Conceivably, he could "pull rank" and say, "I am the head of this house. I make the final decisions around here. Therefore, we are going to Gander Mountain."

Anybody who has been married any length of time will know such foolishness will quickly lead to the opposite of a celestial marriage. The husband in such a scenario might be technically correct, but in the greater spectrum of a marriage, having such an attitude is unwise. Obviously, some sort of middle ground needs to be reached. In this illustration perhaps the solution would be to go to both places.

Paul prefaces the more crucial principles with the advice of cooperating with each other. Submitting or yielding to each other in garden-variety, day-to-day decisions will lubricate the areas where friction might otherwise develop, destroying the tranquillity of a heavenly marriage. The thought in verse 21, in my view, is not so much a major principle. Rather, it is good advice for keeping things on a pleasant plane.

DIVINELY DELEGATED AUTHORITY

We come to a major scriptural principle in marriage. Paul says that God has established a delegation of authority in the home. That authority flows from Jesus Christ, through the husband, to the wife.

Before looking at this principle in detail, it may be well to take an overview of God's delegated authority in society. *All authority ultimately comes from God.* God has established three basic institutions in human society: The first is the institution of marriage (or the home). Additionally, God ordained the institution of human government. Though that institution has taken different forms from nation to nation and over the centuries, as a whole it is ordained of God. God has also established the institution of the church, particularly in this age.

In each divinely established institution, God has ordained leadership to which He has delegated authority. In the institution of marriage, that leadership and delegated authority are through the husband. This principle certainly flies in the face of modern feminist ideology, but it is clear in the Bible. The

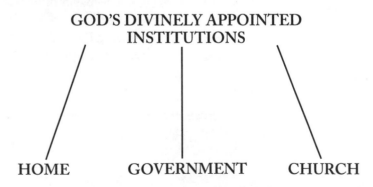

GOD'S DIVINELY APPOINTED INSTITUTIONS

HOME   GOVERNMENT   CHURCH

Bible is the absolute authority for faith and practice, and in it we find clear instruction regarding the leadership of a home.

THE PRINCIPLE OF SUBMISSION

In verse 22 of this chapter, Paul writes, "Wives, submit yourselves unto your own husbands, as unto the Lord."

(1) The verb *submit* is in the imperative mood. That means it is a command. In military jargon, it is an order. Therefore, God has commanded wives to submit to their husbands.

(2) Notice the final phrase of the verse, "as unto the Lord." Submission of a wife to her husband is predicated upon the greater principle that God has delegated leadership and authority to the husband. That does not mean a husband is always right or wise. However, he does occupy a divinely ordained position of leadership which comes from God. Because of the position a husband occupies, he stands in the place of God by virtue of the authority which God has given him.

A policeman is an extension of the authority which God has delegated to the leaders of the nation. The policeman may not always be right or wise in the fulfillment of his duties; nevertheless, he occupies a position that demands the submission of the

> **VOLUNTARY SUBMIS-SION IS A SPIRITUAL ATTITUDE THAT IS ALL-INCLUSIVE.**
>
> IT INVOLVES:
> - Giving in
> - Cooperating
> - Assuming responsibility
> - Sharing the burden

other citizens, as far as the laws of the land are concerned. Likewise, the husband, by virtue of his position, has God-given authority in the leadership of the home. The wife is commanded by God to submit herself to her husband.

(3) The definition of the word translated *submit* is interesting. *Thayer's Greek Lexicon* defines this word: "(1) to subordinate; (2) to put in subjection; (3) to submit oneself or to obey; (4) to submit to one's control; (5) to yield to one's admonition or advice." Thayer continues, "The word was originally a Greek military term meaning to arrange troop divisions in a military fashion under the command of a leader. **In nonmilitary use, it was a voluntary attitude of giving in, cooperating, assuming responsibility, and carrying a burden**" (emphasis added).

To be sure, a marriage relationship between a husband and a wife is not a military relationship. However, the nonmilitary definition of the word is most helpful. Submission is a *voluntary* attitude of giving in, cooperating, assuming responsibility and carrying a burden. That is a beautiful description of God's ordained plan for the submission of a wife to her husband.

Notice the phrase "a voluntary attitude." The scriptural submission of a wife to her husband begins with a voluntary attitude. I have heard wives say, "Well, he might be the head of the house, and I may have to submit outwardly, but inwardly I am going to do my own thing." There is little submission in such an attitude, and there will be little tranquillity or genuine happiness in such a marriage. That is rebellion, plain and simple. It is the antithesis of what God has commanded in His Word. One will *never* find any heaven on earth in such an attitude.

We all know the adage, "It takes two to fight." If one party in a marriage relationship consistently yields, there will be little fighting, fussing or bickering. By the ordinance of God, the wife is the party who is to submit.

That does not mean she is inferior to her husband. That does not mean he is the dictator. That does not mean he is always right. It does mean God has ordained there is one head of the home. Two-headed creatures are a freak of nature. Moreover, we are touching upon a major principle which is crucial to a celestial marriage. Wives who buck the leadership of their husbands will be unhappy, and their husbands will be unhappy too. Dear wife, accept the role for which God has created you. You will be much happier.

Furthermore, the definition of the word *submit* continues in a voluntary attitude of "giving in." Stubbornness is never a virtue. It is born of pride which breeds contention and strife. As mentioned in the discussion of verse 21, there may be wisdom in mutually yielding to each other in routine matters of everyday life; but when push comes to shove and a major decision has to be made, God has ordained that the husband has this prerogative.

This does not mean the wife may not discuss the matter and share her opinion. (Truly, a wise husband will value the advice and carefully consider the counsel of his wife. A husband who ignores or is cavalier about the counsel of his wife is acting foolishly.) However, somebody has to make the final decision, and God has ordained that it be the husband. A submissive wife will *voluntarily give in.*

The definition of *submission* goes on to include a voluntary attitude of "cooperation." Running around pouting, carrying a chip on your shoulder because you did not get your way, is not only immature, it certainly is not genuine cooperation. I have watched wives pout and be in a snit for days because they did not get their way. The irony of it all is that neither party in the marriage is happy. Not only does the wife make it miserable for her husband, but she also is unhappy. Such marriages are at quite a distance from being heaven on earth.

Finally, the definition of *submission* includes a voluntary attitude of "assuming responsibility and carrying a burden."

Life at times is not easy. When a husband makes a life-changing decision, it may not be easy for the wife. It may mean moving across the country away from family and friends to a new climate and different culture. It may mean the wife's carrying the burden of the home while the husband is away working or assigned to distant military duty. But submission is willingly and voluntarily accepting such burdens and responsibilities. It also is a manifestation of maturity and genuine love.

The key to it all is a wife's *voluntary* attitude of yielding to, obeying and subordinating herself to her husband. There are two major motives for such submission: (1) A godly wife will have *agape* love for her husband; therefore, she will give of herself, yield herself, and voluntarily submit herself to the one she loves. (2) A godly wife will be obedient to God and the clear command of His Word in the structure of a Christian marriage. The command to wives to submit to their husbands is in black and white. It is clear; it is simple. A Christian wife is obligated to obey God.

The Scripture continues by explaining, "For the husband is the head of the wife, even as Christ is the head of the church: and he is the saviour of the body" (vs. 23). Paul elaborates upon the principle of the submission of a wife to her husband as he draws a parallel to the relationship of the church to Jesus Christ. Jesus Christ is the head of the church. He founded it. He shed His blood for it. He established it. It is His and He is the head.

Obviously, a husband has not done the same kind of redemptive work for his wife as Christ as done for the church; nevertheless, Paul essentially equates the husband's leadership and authority to that of Christ. Just as the church is in submission to its head, Jesus Christ, so a wife should be in submission to her husband.

THE RESPONSIBILITY OF LEADERSHIP

Husbands, with whatever prerogative might accompany the privilege of leadership, there also comes a heavy responsibility. God will hold you responsible for everything which goes on in your family. Just as a captain of a ship is responsible for everything happening aboard his ship, so God will hold each husband responsible for what goes on in his family. God will not hold the wife responsible; He will hold the *husband* responsible.

In addition, God will hold you accountable for how your children turn out. If it happens on your watch, fellows, you are responsible to God for it. Someday at the judgment seat of Christ we will give an account of how we led our families. That is a sobering thought.

Moreover, a wise husband will never flaunt his privilege of leadership. Most of us have witnessed some young hotshot who had been given authority. When it was abused and foolishly flaunted, only disrespect and animosity were bred in his subordinates. Husband, be very careful about "pulling rank" on your wife. Though you have that privilege, it would be best to be very careful in how you use it. You will be far wiser and happier always to sit down and talk things over with your wife.

We come back to the more basic matters of *agape* love, friendship, courtesy, kindness, thoughtfulness and being considerate of your wife. Though on the one hand there is a ranking of authority between husband and wife, on the other hand, she is your partner and hopefully your best friend. Including her in your decisions is being considerate and thoughtful of her. It is also important in having a marriage which is heaven on earth.

Treat her as your best friend. Always keep her informed

concerning your thinking on a given matter. You may be right in your decision; but if you are way ahead of your wife in your decision-making process, she may feel left out and ignored. That is not going to help build the warm and wonderful marriage you are seeking. Always talk about matters that pertain to both of you. If you do not keep your wife up-to-date on your decision making, you are being discourteous to and inconsiderate of her. You would not treat a business associate or close friend that way. Leadership requires wise and kind consideration of all involved. That certainly is true of a husband and his wife.

The Apostle Paul concludes his discussion of this principle: "Therefore as the church is subject unto Christ, so let the wives be to their own husbands in every thing" (vs. 24). Several comments are in order: (1) The word *subject* used here is the same word from which the word *submit* is translated. The nuance of the English thought may seem different, but it is the same word in the Greek New Testament. The idea of submission (or subjection) is perhaps stronger in the Scripture than in conventional and contemporary American thought. As the church is subject to Christ, likewise ought wives be to their husbands.

(2) Notice the final phrase, "in every thing." A submissive wife will voluntarily yield herself to her husband in *everything*. Again, that thought flies directly into the face of prevalent feminist philosophy. Nevertheless, the Bible teaches that a submissive Christian wife will obey her husband in everything. Submission is all-inclusive.

It should be noted that there is another biblical principle which may apply here—the precept, "We ought to obey God rather than men" (Acts 5:29). On rare occasion, someone in a position of authority may insist we do something which is contrary to the clear will of God. Though this at first may seem to be a dilemma, the overriding principle is, obedience to God always takes priority over obedience to men.

There are numerous illustrations in the Bible of people's being commanded by duly appointed leadership to do wrong. Whether they were Shadrach, Meshach and Abednego, or Peter in Acts 5:29, or Paul before the Sanhedrin, their decision was simple: they did as God commanded and not what man commanded. When a conflict of priority arose, their obedience was to God.

On very rare occasion, a wife may be asked by her husband to do something she knows is a violation of God's Word. In such cases, she has a command higher than her husband's to follow: that is God's Word. I have known of several situations in which the husbands sought to take their wives barhopping or to wild parties and the wives rightfully refused. But in the vast majority of life experiences, God has enjoined the wife to be in submission to her husband.

THE PRINCIPLE OF *AGAPE* LOVE

In verse 25 the text makes a major shift. The focus is redirected toward the husband and his relationship to his wife. Though Paul takes about thirteen verses to develop the concept, in reality, there are only *two* very simple principles set forth: (1) wives, submit yourselves to your husbands; and, (2) husbands, love your wives. Essentially, that sums up the passage.

God has put the responsibility of love directly upon the husband. Though it certainly might be implied that a wife ought likewise to love her husband, only the husband is *commanded* to love his spouse.

In my view, there are several reasons that only the husband is commanded to love his wife, and not vice versa: (1) With the prerogative of leadership comes the absolute responsibility to love. (2) The male psyche is less predisposed to love than the female; therefore, a man must work at loving. (3) The female psyche is predisposed to love and will tend to reciprocate when love is shown to her. Therefore, the major mandate to love is directed to the husband.

It is evident that God has commanded the husband to love his wife. *Agape* love is by definition "a giving of oneself for another" (in this case, a wife).

Men, as we love our wives, they in turn will *tend* to love us. Therefore, the burden of developing and maintaining a strong love relationship in a marriage falls upon the shoulders of the husband. When a man says he doesn't love his wife anymore, the listener might legitimately wonder if the man has any other sins he cares to confess. The simple fact is, the husband is under orders from God to love his wife.

When a wife complains she doesn't love her husband anymore, in my view the real culprit is the husband—that is, if a husband will love his wife as he ought, she will *tend* to reciprocate that love. Therefore, a husband may need to take inventory of his life pattern and see if there is a full spectrum of the *agape,* selfless love described in the Bible. (See Chapter 4.)

Notice *how* we as husbands are to love our wives: "even as Christ also loved the church, and gave himself for it." Here we have a perfect illustration of the intrinsic meaning of *agape* love. Jesus Christ loved the church (His bride) so much that He gave Himself for her. Furthermore, when we meditate upon Christ's giving Himself, we may gain a limited understanding of the depth of the meaning of *agape* love: He gave His life. Jesus said, "Greater love hath no man than this, that a man lay down his life for his friends" (John 15:13). If a man's wife is his friend, the greatest demonstration of love he could ever make for her is to give his life for her. Sadly, many men won't give of their time, their priorities, their affection or their interests—much less of themselves—for their wives.

Husband, *agape* love is a giving of yourself. Since Jesus Christ loved you so much He gave His life for you, is it not a small thing for you to give your time, interest, affection and kindness to your wife?

Proverbs 10:12 says, "Love covereth all sins." Husband, if you will love your wife as you ought, she is going to overlook your faults. You love her as you ought, and she in due season is not going to nag and criticize you as she does. I am convinced most marriage problems are rooted in the fact that husbands do not love their wives as they ought.

> **Most marriage problems are rooted in the fact that husbands do not love their wives as they ought.**

Even when the wife is self-centered, that condition can be mitigated by a husband who exercises *agape* love as he ought. Moreover, it is far easier for a wife to be submissive to a husband who without question is loving to her.

As detailed in some of the stories earlier in this book, men who are selfish and self-focused are often at the root of unhappy marriages. A man who truly loves his wife will never be unfaithful to her. A man who truly loves his wife will not leave her "high and dry" while he pursues his selfish interests. A man who loves his wife as he ought will never abuse her.

MORE ON HOW TO LOVE

The apostle continued the discussion of how a husband should love his wife: "So ought men to love their wives as their own bodies. He that loveth his wife loveth himself" (vs. 28). Each of us has a God-given instinct of self-preservation. Every one of us has an instinctive concern for his body.

This instinct is also quite evident in animals. When my

Dalmatian dog has a sore paw or any other injury, she is very protective of the wounded area. If I seek to touch her sore or intrude upon her when her body is wounded, she becomes very testy. Most veterinarians understand how delicate it is to treat a wounded animal. Animals are very protective of their bodies, and so are we.

Men, God says that we are to love our wives as much as we love our own bodies. Naturally and instinctively we take steps to protect and nurse ourselves if injured or ill. We will go out of our way to take care of our bodies. We are to love our wives in like manner.

We find here an allusion to the Golden Rule. Jesus said, "And as ye would that men should do to you, do ye also to them likewise" (Luke 6:31). Treat your wife as you would have her treat you. Be as considerate and patient with her as you would have her be with you. Be as selfless and helpful to her as you expect her to be toward you.

It would be good for many husbands to stand back and view themselves and realize how selfish, immature and boorish they can be. I remember a situation in which a fellow just couldn't understand why his wife wanted out of their marriage. He provided well for the family; but his open and adulterous flirtations with other women so humiliated his wife, she could not take it any longer. She finally (though wrongfully) treated him like he had been treating her.

NOURISHING AND CHERISHING

"For no man ever yet hated his own flesh; but nourisheth and cherisheth it, even as the Lord the church."—Vs. 29.

The truth is, we nourish and cherish our bodies. The word translated "cherisheth" has the literal sense "to cherish with tender love or to foster with tender care." That's how we as men are to love our wives, with tender love and tender care.

When I was in fifth grade, I fell and broke my arm. It was obviously broken. My wrist had two ninety-degree bends in it. It was late winter, and I had on a winter jacket. As I made my way home, I carried my broken wrist in my partially unzipped jacket. I nourished and cherished it. It was gingerly, tenderly and carefully carried.

Though prosaic, hopefully this illustrates the idea of how we ought to love our wives. We should love them as Jesus Christ loves the church and tenderly and lovingly provides for His people.

THE PERMANENCY OF MARRIAGE

"For this cause shall a man leave his father and mother, and shall be joined unto his wife, and they two shall be one flesh."—Vs. 31.

There is an interesting nuance in the word here translated "joined." It literally has the sense of being glued or welded together. I think this is a clear implication of God's view of the permanency of marriage. When we get married, as far as God is concerned, we have been glued together. The whole spectrum of our marriage should be so construed: body, soul and spirit. We have been glued and welded together.

THE PRINCIPLE OF RESPECT

"Nevertheless let every one of you in particular so love his wife even as himself; and the wife see that she reverence her husband."—Vs. 33.

The Apostle Paul here summarizes this entire section. Verse 32 speaks of Christ and the church. The words translated "in particular" mean "accordingly." Therefore, the sentence could be rendered, 'Nevertheless let every one of you accordingly so love his wife.' The word *accordingly* refers directly back to verse 32 where Paul spoke of the relationship of Christ and the church. We are to love our wives accordingly.

Once again the verb *to love* here is in the imperative mood. Men, *once more* we are commanded of God to love our wives even as we love ourselves.

Finally, the Holy Spirit concludes with the comment, "and the wife see that she reverence her husband." The word translated "reverence" is the common Greek word for *fear*. It is used in the positive sense of rendering respect.

Let me illustrate it this way: Though we may not *fear* a police officer in the sense that we think he is going to harm us, we of necessity *respect* the authority he possesses.

Some years ago, I was not paying particular attention to what I was doing as I drove down the road. When I looked up, I saw the flashing lights of a patrol car in my mirror. When the officer walked up, he said, "May I see your driver's license, please."

I timidly said, "Yes sir."

"Do you know you rolled through that stop sign back there without coming to a complete stop?"

"No sir."

"Do you know the sticker on your license plate is on the wrong corner?"

"No sir."

"Well, next time make sure you put it on right."

"Yes sir."

"Well, I am just going to give you a warning ticket."

"Thank you, sir."

Throughout that episode, of necessity I was respectful to that police officer. I feared he was going to give me a ticket which would have cost me money. I therefore "reverenced" him.

That is the idea implicit in the word "reverence" in Ephesians 5:33. The word does not necessarily mean that a wife ought to go about always saying "sir" to her husband, but it certainly does convey the idea that a wife should be respectful to her husband and the God-given authority resident within him.

In summary, Ephesians 5:21–33 clearly teaches a wife is to be in submission to her husband. This submission is set forth as an imperative. The thought of voluntarily yielding and obeying is coupled with the idea of respect for her husband.

On four different occasions within this passage, men are enjoined to love their wives even as Christ loved the church. Two of those four occasions are commands.

God's plan is quite simple: Wife, *voluntarily submit* to your husband, respecting his God-given authority. Husband, *categorically love* your wife as Jesus Christ loved the church. These two simple principles are absolutely necessary for a marriage to be heaven on earth.

9.

AN EXPOSITION OF
I PETER 3:1-7

In I Peter 3, the apostle deals with the husband and wife relationship. In some ways the passage parallels what Paul wrote to the Ephesians, yet the Holy Spirit inspired Peter to provide additional detail not found in Ephesians 5.

"Likewise, ye wives, be in subjection to your own husbands; that, if any obey not the word, they also may without the word be won by the conversation of the wives;

"While they behold your chaste conversation coupled with fear.

"Whose adorning let it not be that outward adorning of plaiting the hair, and of wearing of gold, or of putting on of apparel;

"But let it be the hidden man of the heart, in that which is not corruptible, even the ornament of a meek and quiet spirit, which is in the sight of God of great price.

"For after this manner in the old time the holy women also, who trusted in God, adorned themselves, being in subjection unto their own husbands:

"Even as Sara obeyed Abraham, calling him lord: whose daughters ye are, as long as ye do well, and are not afraid with any amazement.

"Likewise, ye husbands, dwell with them according to knowledge, giving honour unto the wife, as unto the weaker vessel, and as being heirs together of the grace of life; that your prayers be not hindered."—
I Pet. 3:1-7.

The chapter begins with the word "likewise"; therefore, the opening paragraph of chapter 3 is linked with the final thoughts of the preceding chapter: (1) "that we...should live unto righteousness" (2:24); (2) that we are now turned (in submission) to the Shepherd and Bishop of our souls (2:25). This, of course, is Jesus Christ. The word *bishop* in its generic sense basically means "the leader or the head of a given group."

THE WINNING OF A HUSBAND

"Likewise, ye wives, be in subjection to your own husbands" (I Pet. 3:1). The evident thought is that even as God's people have turned to Christ as their leader and head, likewise the wife ought be in submission to the leadership of her husband. The principle is the same as it is in Ephesians 5:22. Moreover, the Greek word translated *subjection* in I Peter 3:1 is the very same word that is translated *submit* in Ephesians 5:22.

Peter goes on to point out that genuine submission of a Christian wife to her unsaved husband may be the means of winning him to Christ.

Several possible alternative thoughts are also in view. The winning of a husband may not refer to reaching him for Christ but to winning the love and loyalty for his wife he ought to have—that is, the winning of a drifting husband.

A. T. Robertson, the noted New Testament Greek expert, suggests the phrase, "without the word," is not a reference to the Word of God but rather to a wife's tongue. That is, the gracious, submissive behavior of a godly woman can win over her husband when her nagging will not. Furthermore, the nagging and preaching of a wife more often than not are counterproductive.

However, when a godly woman will be submissive in her overall deportment to her husband, she can be a powerful influence upon him. The word translated "conversation" has the sense of "one's total behavior, decorum and deportment." It could also be called one's lifestyle.

In the following verses, Peter more fully develops this idea. A godly Christian woman will be submissive to the lordship of Jesus Christ in her life. She also will be genuinely submissive to her husband in her behavior, attitude and deportment. In so doing, she will have a profound influence on her husband.

The principle of submission is not only a part of the recipe for a happy marriage, it is also a prerequisite for spiritually touching the heart of a husband.

CHASTITY AND REVERENCE

In addition to the principle of submission, Peter adds two other virtues when he speaks of a wife whose "conversation" is "chaste...coupled with fear." The word *conversation* suggests decorum, behavior and deportment; but the Holy Spirit adds the qualification of being *chaste*. Though this word certainly suggests sexual fidelity, it actually refers to the whole spectrum of being pure, morally and spiritually. (See II Corinthians 7:1.) The Greek word used for *chaste* is derived from the more basic word used for *holiness*. A woman who is pure, not only in her morals but throughout her entire spirit, is profoundly attractive to her husband.

Verse 2 is actually part of the uncompleted thought of verse 1, which speaks of winning a husband. In completing the thought, Peter alludes to "fear." The thought is quite similar to that in Ephesians 5:33 where Paul referred to the wife's giving "reverence" to her husband. The greater concept is *respect*.

Therefore, the first two verses of this chapter speak of submission, purity and gracious respect in every area of the life of the wife. These attributes can deeply affect her husband and his attitude toward her.

GENUINE BEAUTY

In verses 3 and 4 the apostle continues on a related path—that is, the real source of genuine beauty in a Christian woman is internal and not external. It is spiritual and not physical. There is nothing wrong with outward beauty or physical attractiveness. Unfortunately, not everyone is so endowed; but *everyone* can be beautiful spiritually, and spiritual beauty is indeed attractive.

Years ago I saw a political cartoon which conveyed an obviously attractive woman. In the next frame, though fully clothed and otherwise proper, she was standing in front of an old-fashioned X-ray fluoroscope which revealed the skeletal structure and internal organs of her abdomen. The X ray revealed the normal anatomical structure beneath the surface of the human body, and there is not much attractiveness about that. The caption on the cartoon was "Beauty is only skin deep."

The truth is, however, real beauty is deep. It emanates from our spirit. (The issues of life are fundamentally spiritual.)

"Whose adorning let it not be that outward adorning of plaiting the hair, and of wearing of gold, or of putting on of apparel;

"But let it be the hidden man of the heart, in that which is not corruptible, even the ornament of a meek and quiet spirit, which is in the sight of God of great price."—Vss. 3, 4.

The Bible says the real beauty of a woman ought to be internal and not external. Peter is not saying it is wrong for a woman to fix her hair or wear jewelry. Rather, he is building a case: genuine attractiveness is primarily spiritual and not physical. Genuine adorning or beauty is not skin-deep. It is internal. Age will not disfigure it. In fact, age will only enhance it.

> **Genuine attractiveness is primarily spiritual, not physical.**

Genuine beauty is not in a fancy hairdo. The phrase "plaiting the hair" means just that. There is nothing wrong with a nice hairdo, but Peter says this is not where *real* beauty lies. Neither is it in "wearing of gold, or of putting on of apparel." Peter is not condemning such. Rather, he is teaching genuine beauty lies neither in jewelry nor fancy clothes.

We live in a culture which has taught that attractiveness lies in beauty of face, hair and form. Moreover, we have been conditioned to believe that true beauty may be achieved by embellishing physical features through jewelry, hairdo and clothing. There is nothing wrong with being appropriately attractive. However, this is not where real beauty lies.

Probably all have witnessed women who were outwardly and physically attractive. However, in getting to know them, we found they were very unattractive in spirit.

I remember an individual who was quite attractive outwardly; but she was moody, often pouting. Once she was crossed, she became a witch. This young woman had attracted her husband by her physical features; but her physical attractiveness soon wore thin as she whined, pouted and lashed out at her husband with her tongue. Their marriage was not happy.

Perhaps the classic tale in modern history of two physically beautiful people who turned out to be profoundly miserable is that of Prince Charles and Princess Diana of England. Even with no comment on who was at fault in that debacle, the couple illustrates the point at hand. He was the world's foremost bachelor, handsome in his royal decorum. She was the strikingly beautiful Cinderella. But neither lived happily ever after, and both were very openly and in well-documented manner utterly miserable. Physical beauty adds little in developing a marriage which is heaven on earth. It may even be a deterrent.

Our text speaks of the "hidden man" (vs. 4). That may

seem incongruous inasmuch as Peter is talking about wives here. (To any gender-sensitive readers, Peter's choice of words is generic.) He is referring to the internal or inner person *of the heart*. He is indirectly referring to a wife's spirit, particularly how she relates to her husband. In the flow of the context, Peter is in effect saying, "Wives, let not your primary beauty be external, but internal." Genuine beauty begins in the heart of a godly wife.

There is deeper meaning in the words Peter chose to use. The word "adorning" in verses 3 through 5 comes from the Greek word *kosmos*. It is the word from which our common English words *cosmetic* and *cosmopolitan* are derived. (It is also the word most commonly translated "world" in the New Testament.) That which is cosmetic is outward and generally shallow.

Moreover, in the Bible the word *kosmos* is more than a passing reference to the world. In any event, in this context it is used to refer to outward beautification. In contrast, the hidden person of the heart is spiritual, internal and deep.

A little proverb in the North country is "Still water runs deep." I am thinking of two currents of water in the Northland. One is shallow. It babbles and gushes as it rushes over the rocks of its stream bed on its way to Lake Superior. It is pretty to look at, but because of its shallowness it is not very good for drinking. Moreover, the level of this stream often fluctuates, depending upon recent rainfall.

The other current of water is in a deeply forested canyon. In mirrorlike fashion it serenely flows to its destination. Its waters, though not so dynamic and photogenic, are clean, clear, cold and sweet. The one water is good for a picture; the other is pure and life-sustaining. Still water runs deep.

The genuine beauty of a gracious, spiritual woman is deep.

The phrase, "in that which is not corruptible," adds to the word picture being developed. The hidden man of the heart (our spirit) is not corruptible. Physical beauty fades with age. The striking beauty of a young woman in her prime over the years will fade, even as a lovely flower will fade with time. The world therefore adds cosmetics to give a new "paint job" to the faded beauty she once enjoyed.

Ironically, the beauty of a quiet, gracious spirit which "runs deep" does not fade with time. In fact, as a person matures, such beauty becomes even more appealing. Physical beauty fades with the passing of time; spiritual beauty grows as time progresses.

"A MEEK AND QUIET SPIRIT"

In addition, Peter qualifies the internal spiritual beauty of a gracious, godly woman with more descriptive words, "a meek and quiet spirit." In the view of this author, one of the most misunderstood words in the Bible is the word *meek* or *meekness*. The common idea of a *meek* person is that he is a mousy, timid individual who allows everyone to run over him. That is absolutely not the meaning of the word used in the Greek New Testament. The word implies a gentle spirit which results from the control or discipline of one's emotions. A meek person will not allow his or her temper or other emotions to flare up on provocation. They are under control. A meek person has a gentle spirit and disposition.

Gentleness or meekness is the opposite of self-assertiveness and self-interest. It stems from trust in God's goodness and God's control over any situation at hand. A meek person is not occupied with self. Meekness is a mature development of the fruit of the Spirit mentioned in Galatians 5:23. It is an eminently spiritual virtue. With meekness, the God-given new nature disciplines and overrides impulses of emotion and outward reaction to life's events.

151

Meekness emanating from our spirits will keep us cool, calm and collected. It will preempt emotional outbursts, preclude loss of temper, restrain a retaliatory tongue, and subdue a bitter and vindictive attitude. Meekness is closely related to spiritual maturity. It will throttle the selfish interests of the old nature. In short, it is a significant spiritual quality.

It is germane at this point to note that Jesus Christ called Himself meek (Matt. 11:29). Being Christlike involves developing meekness. It is a definite spiritual virtue for a wife. It will add grace and depth to a marriage relationship.

Meekness is coupled with a quiet spirit. The sense of the word *quiet* is "being tranquil or peaceable." This contradicts the prevalent contemporary feminist doctrine of women's being self-assertive, aggressive and outspoken.

"It is better to dwell in a corner of the housetop, than with a brawling woman in a wide house" (Prov. 21:9). The word translated "brawling" has the sense of "being contentious." It is practically the opposite of having a quiet spirit.

"It is better to dwell in the wilderness, than with a contentious and an angry woman" (vs. 19). Solomon described the attitude which is opposite of the "meek and quiet spirit" described by Peter. God's Word is consistent and factual. A wife's having "a meek and quiet spirit" adds immeasurably to the probability that a marriage will be a heaven on earth.

MORE ON INTERNAL BEAUTY

The Apostle Peter says that such internal beauty—"a meek and quiet spirit"—is "in the sight of God of great price." In other words, God considers it priceless. It is of great value. Dear Christian wife, if you would build a marriage which is heaven on earth, God's instruction for you is inspired, and it works.

"For after this manner in the old time the holy women also, who trusted in God, adorned themselves, being in subjection unto their own husbands."—I Pet. 3:5.

Not only is the matter of subjection (submission) brought up again, it is set forth in the context of spiritual beauty. Real and lasting beauty is internal and not external. It is spiritual and not physical.

Peter alludes to biblical history in reiterating the point. Godly women of bygone eras beautified themselves before their husbands by being in submission to them.

"Even as Sara obeyed Abraham, calling him lord: whose daughters ye are, as long as ye do well, and are not afraid with any amazement."—Vs. 6.

Peter refers to one of those holy women from the past, namely Sarah. The Holy Spirit inspired Peter simply to comment that she obeyed her husband. If immediate context has any connection to the thought under consideration (and it usually does), then Sarah was also a submissive wife. There is every reason to believe she possessed that gracious and elegant apparel of "a meek and quiet spirit" so necessary to a wonderful marriage.

Another interesting comment is made here. The Scripture, in commenting on Sarah's relationship to her husband, says that she was in the habit of "calling him lord." A more contemporary rendering of the word *lord* might be *sir*. Perhaps a part of this matter is rooted in the culture of the day; nevertheless, what remains obvious is that Sarah was respectful and courteous to her husband.

We come back to the previously discussed principle of respect for the husband. Such decorum and courtesy are appropriate inasmuch as: (1) the husband is the God-ordained leader of the home; (2) on a practical level, courtesy and respect are ingredients which are a part of common decency; (3) the "honey" in the honeymoon needed for a marriage which is heaven on earth will not be perpetual if there are not ongoing courtesy and respect. No doubt the husband should be courteous and respectful toward the wife, but the Bible exhorts particularly the wife in this regard.

WISE HUSBANDS

In verse 7 Peter speaks to husbands: "Likewise, ye husbands, dwell with them according to knowledge, giving honour unto the wife, as unto the weaker vessel, and as being heirs together of the grace of life; that your prayers be not hindered."

The portion dealing with husbands begins with a "likewise," just as did the earlier portion of the chapter concerning wives. If we would follow the logic of that point, the *likewise* here refers to the end of chapter 2. In the opinion of this author, Peter is likely referring to the admonition in I Peter 2:24, that we "should live unto righteousness." If that is the case, then Peter is admonishing husbands to do right by their wives. What he advises surely is righteous.

The injunction here is for husbands to dwell or live with their wives according to knowledge. That command could be paraphrased, "Husbands, live with your wives in wisdom."

According to A. T. Robertson, the grammatical construction is essentially that of an imperative. In other words, this is a command for husbands from God's Word.

The book of Proverbs is God's book of wisdom. In it wisdom is defined and applied to the day-to-day matters of life. In Proverbs 8 wisdom is essentially equated with righteousness. That is, to do what is right is to do what is wise; conversely, to do wisely is to do what is right.

In the same chapter, Wisdom is personified:

"Doth not wisdom cry? and understanding put forth her voice?"

*"Hear; for I will speak of excellent things; and the opening of my lips shall be **right** things.*

"For my mouth shall speak truth; and wickedness is an abomination to my lips.

*"All the words of my mouth are in **righteousness**; there is nothing froward or perverse in them."*

*"I lead in the way of **righteousness**, in the midst of the paths of judgment."*—Prov. 8:1, 6–8, 20.

Notice how Wisdom personified leads in the way of righteousness. That is, Wisdom takes the lead in doing what is *right*. Furthermore, the opening of the lips of Wisdom is in *right* things and *right* words. A wise husband will do what is right. He will lead in the right direction and will frame his words in righteousness.

This teaching concerning wisdom may be considered with the admonition given husbands in I Peter 3:7. Husbands who "dwell with them according to knowledge" are husbands who are wise in their relationships with their wives. In the light of Proverbs 8, they are husbands who will do right by their wives.

Mr. Husband, you have the prerogative of leadership; therefore, you should do what is right by your wife, for your wife and to your wife. Wisdom leads in the way of righteousness. A wise husband will lead his wife and family to do what is right.

A husband who leads according to knowledge (that is, wisely) will always be careful to sift his words through the filter of righteousness. A wise husband will not use sharp, coarse or unkind language. Moreover, as Chapter 6 of this book discusses, it is righteousness which is the foundation for peace in a marriage. Peace is the prerequisite for happiness.

Mr. Husband, with whatever privilege you may have in

being the head of your house comes the concomitant responsibility to be a wise, upright leader. God has called you to live wisely with your wife. That means doing what is right in every area of your life but particularly in specifics relating to your wife and her happiness. Be wise. Live with your wife according to knowledge. Always do right to her, for her and by her.

HONORING YOUR WIFE

The next phrase is "giving honour unto the wife." There is a profound principle here which every husband needs to learn. We are commanded of God to honor our wives. Fellows, since God has given you the prerogative of being the masters of your houses, you should be aware that your wives are the queens; and you need to treat them as such.

The sense of the verb *to honor* literally means "to give deference to one who is deserving by reason of rank or office." The idea borders on worship. Husband, the truth is, your wife is the queen of your home. Treat her as such. She is worthy of it.

TREAT YOUR WIFE AS QUEEN

There are several ways in which you ought to honor your wife:

1. Compliment her. There is always something about which you might compliment your wife. It may be small or it may be large, but honor her by complimenting her. No wife is perfect; but I will assure you, your wife has many little areas which are worthy of compliment. Such may be her cooking, her appearance, her housekeeping, her wisdom, her modesty, her thoughtfulness, her kindness, and/or her romantic charm. But compliment her. Praise her. Let her know you are proud of her and thankful for her.

It is good to do these things in private, but it is even better to let others know what a wonderful wife you think she is. Praise your wife before your children. Tell them what a wonderful mother they have. Let your in-laws know how appreciative you are of their daughter. Brag on her in front of your family. Let them know what a fine wife she is. In their presence mention some attributes of your wife for which you are thankful. To honor her is to praise and compliment her (especially before others).

2. Thank her. Your wife ought to be your best friend. Honor her by letting her know how appreciative you are of her. It is appropriate to thank her for her good work, for a good meal, for doing your laundry. Never sink into the rut of the attitude, "Well, that's her job." Maybe it is; but thank her for doing the housework, for taking care of whatever little chore needed to be done, for being a good mother to your children, for being a good lover.

3. Give gifts to her. Stop to think: *Generally, when a person is honored, what usually accompanies the honor? A gift.* Beware you do not forget such dates as birthdays and anniversaries. However, it is always in order to bring home a little gift for your wife. It may be as simple as a card, or a modest bouquet of flowers, or even a single rose. As family finances allow, it may be more expensive. But honor her by giving to her.

On occasion, take her out to eat. Honoring your wife is not an optional suggestion in the Bible: it is essentially an imperative. God says to do it. Put on your thinking cap and figure out little ways to honor her. Even as royalty honors other royalty by giving gifts, so honor your wife.

4. Help her. The male chauvinist thinks housework is

the wife's job and therefore not his responsibility. But, Husband, helping your wife around the house is not being a profeminist, role-reversal house-husband. You may protest you come home after a hard day's work; but there is certain truth in the old axiom, "A woman's work is never done." In the world in which we live, it seems wives are either home taking care of the children or helping earn family income by working out of the home. Both put loads on them.

Honor your wife by helping her. It may mean doing the dishes, changing the baby's diaper, helping with the laundry, making the bed and cleaning up the bedroom, doing the grocery shopping, running the vacuum or helping with the cooking. Don't misunderstand: I am not suggesting that these are things which you as husband ought to be doing regularly. What I am suggesting is that these are ways you may honor your wife by helping her.

Honor your wife! Be thoughtful of her. Think of ways to lift her spirit. Put her on a pedestal. Treat her as the queen of the home. Give deference to her. Show her affection. Be thoughtful of her. This is another demonstration of *agape* love. Husband, honor your wife. Doing so will help make marriage for both of you a heaven on earth.

"…as unto the weaker vessel" (vs. 7). Peter is simply saying that the wife usually is not as physically strong as the husband. That should be obvious, but the modern feminist movement is unwilling to acknowledge the fact that there are no women playing NFL football. It is not because of some male bigotry or discrimination; it is simply because, generally speaking, women are physically weaker than men.

In the context of the admonishment for a husband to be wise, honoring his wife, there is the implication that the husband should share in the work load in the home. The wife in no way is inferior to her husband intellectually or spiritually. She may even be superior in those areas. However, a man will not only be wise in helping his wife with the work, but in so doing he will also honor her and demonstrate his love for her.

HEIRS OF THE GRACE OF LIFE

Moreover, husbands are enjoined to live wisely with their wives and honor them because they are "heirs together of the grace of life." God has intended marriage be permanent. There are numerous reasons for that, but one is that, over the long haul, a married couple become heirs together of the grace of life. The things which are really important in life are not money, career and advancement. (Ironically, some believe they are. However, as life progresses, such things become empty, leaving a person lonely.)

Children are a grace of life. As our children develop and grow up, they are a grace of life. As they marry and have children, there is the grace of grandchildren. A happy retirement is a grace of life. Memories of happy bygone days are a grace of life. Memories of all the various stages of development of our children are a grace of life. The completion of projects accomplished jointly by husband and wife is a grace of life. (My wife and I, along with our children, built our home together. It is something of which we are proud. It is one grace in our lives.) The little things which are warm and memorable are the grace of life.

Peter advises, 'Husband, you had better be wise in how you live with your wife. You had better honor her and help her; for if you are not careful, you may miss out on major blessings in life.'

As a pastor I have witnessed the loneliness and emptiness of men who, because of their folly and thoughtlessness, lost their wives to divorce or emotional estrangement.

Fellows, the older you get, the more you will come to appreciate the little graces of life. Your wives have probably enjoyed them all along, even if you have ignored them; but someday you will long for those things. A wise and thoughtful husband will invest in an inheritance which will be bestowed later in life—the grace of life. It is fragile and easily lost. Therefore, Peter counsels wisdom and deference in the marriage relationship.

Sadly, many a couple miss the fullness of this grace through the tragedy of divorce. Apart from the moral or ethical ramifications concerning divorce, it is foolish. There will never be a full realization of the grace of life a couple might have inherited had they maintained a happy marriage.

HINDERED PRAYER

Peter warns that failure to follow these principles may well result in hindered prayer. The Bible teaches that prayer is a privilege which belongs to those who have a relationship with God through Jesus Christ. It is a wonderful and powerful privilege. Not only is it a primary means of having fellowship with God, but it also allows unlimited access to God's power and riches.

Yet the Bible teaches there is one thing which will short-circuit our prayer system. That is sin. When we willfully and knowingly allow sin in our lives, the antenna of our prayer life is de-tuned. It won't work anymore. Sin fouls up the transmitter of our prayer life. We can pray into the microphone all we want, but the transmitter has been de-tuned. God will not hear our prayer.

"If I regard iniquity in my heart, the Lord will not hear me" (Ps. 66:18). This verse says simply that when I allow sin in my life, God will not listen to my prayer. Isaiah 59:1 and 2 sets forth a similar thought:

> *"Behold, the LORD'S hand is not shortened, that it cannot save; neither his ear heavy, that it cannot hear:*
>
> *"But your iniquities have separated between you and your God, and your sins have hid his face from you, that he will not hear."*

The problem is not that God *cannot* hear our prayer but that when sin is allowed in our lives, He *will not* hear.

Husband, failing to treat your wife right is a sin which will shut down the power of your prayer life. Your prayer won't make it through the attic.

Lest you think this is of little consequence, the day may be coming when you are desperately going to need to use the spiritual "9-1-1" in your life but the prayer line will be down. You may be in the visitors' room of the intensive care unit of your local hospital as the doctors work on your child. Because of the sin of dealing unrighteously with your wife, your prayer won't make it through the ceiling tile. It may be you will plead with God to spare your elderly parent, but the sin of failing to honor your wife as you ought will have short-circuited your prayer line. It is a serious thing for a husband to deal "unseemly" (I Cor. 13:5) with his wife. God takes note of it.

In summary, God has enjoined a Christian wife to be in submission to her husband, beautifying herself internally with a meek and quiet spirit. God has commanded the husband to live wisely and righteously with his wife, honoring and helping her. There are wide-ranging blessings which will affect the rest of the lives of the husbands and wives who obey these commands. These virtues are major ingredients to a celestial marriage.

10.

AN EXPOSITION OF
I CORINTHIANS 7:1–6

First Corinthians 7 is an interesting chapter in that in it the Apostle Paul is replying to questions the Corinthian church had written to him. (Paul had gone to Corinth, won people to Christ, established the church, and in due season gone elsewhere. Because they did not have the complete New Testament, Paul replied to the Corinthian Christians in the epistle which we now call I Corinthians.) Though we do not know the exact questions Paul was asked, his answers give fairly good indication as to what they might have been.

In this chapter, he deals with physical intimacy in marriage, problems in marriage, divorce and even remarriage. It is not the purpose of this book to examine the entire spectrum of marriage problems, much less divorce or remarriage. Our focus is upon what the Bible teaches concerning how to have a wonderful marriage. If God's people would have the type of marriages God intended, the problems of divorce and remarriage would be virtually eliminated.

"Now concerning the things whereof ye wrote unto me: It is good for a man not to touch a woman.

"Nevertheless, to avoid fornication, let every man have his own wife, and let every woman have her own husband.

"Let the husband render unto the wife due benevolence: and likewise also the wife unto the husband.

"The wife hath not power of her own body, but the husband: and likewise also the husband hath not power of his own body, but the wife.

"Defraud ye not one the other, except it be with consent for a time, that ye may give yourselves to fasting and prayer; and come together again, that Satan tempt you not for your incontinency.

"But I speak this by permission, and not of commandment."—
I Cor. 7:1–6.

PAGAN CUSTOMS

Evidently, a question posed to Paul by the Corinthian church pertained to men's relationships with women. Corinth was a prosperous, cosmopolitan port city located on a narrow isthmus of land in southern Greece. Because of its location between the Aegean and Adriatic Seas, it was a major seaport with commerce going both directions across the narrow isthmus. As is often true in seaports, general prostitution was common in Corinth.

Part of the pagan religion prevalent in Corinth involved institutional temple prostitution. The depraved idolatry of the day taught that when the gods observed immorality at the temple, they would be aroused to send fertility to the land. When the pagans went to the temple at Corinth, they were intimate with temple prostitutes. Needless to say, Corinth was a city of promiscuity.

Living in that environment, this young church of new Christians had written Paul evidently asking if Christians should participate in any such conduct. Paul replied by setting forth a basic principle that members of opposite sexes should in general avoid physical contact with each other. This is obviously not directed to married people. Otherwise, the basic principle stands: With the exception of members of our immediate family, we ought to keep our hands off members of the opposite sex. There is genuine wisdom in this injunction.

GOD'S BASIC PLAN

"Nevertheless, to avoid fornication, let every man have his own wife, and let every woman have her own husband."—Vs. 2.

Paul kills two birds with one stone: (1) for some, celibacy has been presumed to be a more spiritual or a godlier way of living. In I Timothy 4:1–3, Paul says that in the last days one mark of apostasy will be a forbidding to marry. God ordained marriage and the physical intimacy which takes place therein (Heb. 13:4).

(2) However, Paul touches upon a more day-to-day matter: marriage, with its normal and natural physical intimacy, is a major preclusion to immorality. The Greek word translated "fornication" is interesting. It is *porneia*. Our English word *pornography* is derived from it. In its narrower meaning, it refers to premarital intimate relations. The world has all kinds of euphemisms, such as "living together" or "sleeping together." The Bible calls it fornication.

However, in the broader sense of the word, it can refer to any impure or wrongful intimate relationships. It may refer to adultery, prostitution, homosexuality, incest, bestiality or any other kind of sexual activity outside the marriage relationship. Therefore, Paul is in effect saying, to avoid immorality of any type, let each man or woman have his or her respective spouse.

Though there *never* is any justification for adultery, people at times do resort to extramarital relationships because their spouses will not cooperate. Because I am a pastor, people have told me that they have resorted to impure methods because their spouses would not be intimate with them. In other cases, people of both sexes have told me of their having "affairs" because their needs were not being met at home. That does not in any way justify errant behavior, but such instances *do* happen because of such "reasons."

In even more tragic cases, I have known of people who have engaged in immoral criminal activity because they were denied having their needs met by their spouses. Again, that is no justification or mitigation of such behavior. It is sin, plain and simple. It is wrong! But it *does* happen.

God has ordained the marriage relationship as normal, healthy and desirable. In essence, verse 2 in its context teaches that a significant deterrent to immorality is a healthy and fulfilling marriage.

But not only is this a means of precluding improper activity, it surely is a significant ingredient to a marriage which is warm and wonderful. God has created our secret parts not only for procreation but also for the deepest of intimacy and physical pleasure. A husband and wife who are completely at home and totally enraptured with each other know some of the significance of the idea of a marriage which is celestial.

Clearly, physical intimacy within the marriage relationship is encouraged by the Scripture, which also seems to imply that such is for more than procreation. As a general principle, the Bible teaches marriage is for meeting physical needs and for pleasure, as well as for procreation. (See Proverbs 5:18–20.)

First Corinthians 7 presents basic advice to the husband and wife. Herein lies godly advice for not only maintaining morality but also for drawing a couple into the deepest of intimacy. It is the view of this author that a marriage which is heaven on earth can hardly be realized without the kind of intimate physical relationship which God designed a married couple should have. (For exceptional cases where persons are incapacitated through poor health or accident, the special grace of God can still make the marriage a heaven on earth.)

THE PRINCIPLE OF KINDNESS

"Let the husband render unto the wife due benevolence: and likewise also the wife unto the husband."—Vs. 3.

The location of verse 3 in the context is curious. (A basic principle of hermeneutics—the science of interpretation—is that context is a major factor in determining the understanding of a given text.) In the context both preceding and succeeding this verse, Paul is clearly discussing physical intimacy in marriage. That would lead us to conclude that verse 3 is at least related to the greater context—physical intimacy in marriage.

However, before considering the connection of this verse to its surrounding context, let us look at the truth intrinsic in the verse itself. Husbands are commanded by the Scripture to render unto their wives due benevolence; likewise, the wives, to their husbands. The word *benevolence* has the sense of "kindness" or of "good will." Moreover, the apostle says such kindness or benevolence is due or owed. That is, we owe it to our spouses. They deserve such treatment.

Kindness is a direct function of *agape* love. When we love our spouses as God has commanded us, we will in fact be kind to them. Kindness and benevolence are due because we have been commanded to love our spouses. This is particularly true for husbands. "And as ye would that men should do to you, do ye also to them likewise" (Luke 6:31). The principle taught in the Golden Rule is simple: We must demonstrate to others the kindness which we would like to receive. This begins at home with our spouses. Because we should treat our spouses in accordance with the Golden Rule, we owe such kindness to our spouses. It is "due benevolence."

Though any spouse has his faults, he does much for his mate and therefore deserves kindness and benevolence. Because of the laundry and cooking your wife does for you or because she has borne your children, she deserves your kindness, my friend. Because of the husband's care for the car and the house or because of the paycheck he lays on the table, he deserves kindness from his wife.

God has commanded both husbands and wives to be kind to their spouses. Kindness is the opposite of nagging, of being inconsiderate, of sarcasm, selfishness and immaturity. It is the opposite of pouting, of losing your temper, of calling each other names or of not forgiving. It is the opposite of dredging up past problems and of harboring bitterness and animosity.

Kindness is being thoughtful of your spouse, being helpful, having a sweet spirit, being submissive to the wishes of your mate, being pleasant, praising and complimenting, thinking of ways to show appreciation, being mature and being selfless. It calls for a good reaction and aftermath. It is lifting the other's spirit, encouraging and being selfless (which is the essence of *agape* love).

Unkind	Kind
🦋 Nagging	❤ Thoughtfulness
🦋 Inconsideration	❤ Helpfulness
🦋 Sarcasm	❤ Sweet-spiritedness
🦋 Selfishness	❤ Submission
🦋 Immaturity	❤ Pleasantness
🦋 Pouting	❤ Praisefulness
🦋 Temper	❤ Compliments
🦋 Name-calling	❤ Appreciation
🦋 Unforgiveness	❤ Maturity
🦋 Rehashing	❤ Selflessness
🦋 Bitterness	❤ Good reaction
🦋 Animosity	❤ Encouragement

God has commanded us to show kindness to our spouses because they deserve it. If you cannot think of any reason why your spouse deserves kindness from you, then it is you who has the problem.

Without a question, a major ingredient of a marriage which is heaven on earth is the simple matter of being kind to one's spouse. It is foundational. You may well try to cobble together all manner of strategies to have a happier marriage; but if you do not develop simple kindness one to another, you will never have a marriage which is heavenly.

Truly an irony of life is that people are often unkind to those who are closest and dearest to them. It is as common as the day is long for husbands and wives to be unkind to each other frequently. The reason is spiritual. (The issues of life remain fundamentally spiritual.) The old nature with which each is born is intrinsically and systemically selfish.

In a coming chapter, we will deal at length with the matter of the old nature and how to get victory over it; but for the sake of discussion at this point, we here state that it is incumbent upon us to work at being kind to our spouses. The more we work at it, the more engrained it will become. Eventually, it will become a habit and part of the fabric of our character. Be kind to your spouse.

Why did the Holy Spirit insert an admonition about being kind into a context dealing with physical intimacy in the marriage relationship? In my view, there is an apparent reason: there is a crucial relationship between the quality and satisfaction of a husband and wife's physical intimacy and how they treat each other the rest of the time.

The world writes and talks frequently about *good sex*. Secular bookstores continually have books on how to have better intimacy. There are all kinds of advice. Secular magazines, particularly for women, routinely have articles on such. They stare at you every time you go through the checkout line at the grocery store. Ironically, though the world has given itself to all manner of fornication and adultery, it is without real fulfillment. For many in the world, there is a lack of genuine enjoyment therein.

"Free love" in the world is for the most part empty, hollow and meaningless. For that crowd, it usually means *quantity* but rarely means *quality* of intimacy or true enjoyment.

In this text God has inserted a little "hidden manna" which is a major key to fulfillment in physical intimacy in the marriage relationship. That key is found in I Corinthians 7:3. It is mutual kindness between husband and wife in the overall marriage relationship.

Many "relationships" in the world are outside the marriage bond and therefore miss the first qualification. Moreover, many in the world's scene care little about being genuinely kind to their "significant others." Ironically, a liberated lifestyle is often empty and mechanical, though many in it claim they have "the ultimate." They miss the other qualification given in the Word of God—that is, kindness.

In the view of this author, there is a direct cause-and-effect correlation between the overall relationship of a couple and their fulfillment in physical intimacy. In the marriage relationship, sexual enjoyment and fulfillment will be directly related to the general rapport and personal relationship between the partners. Fulfillment in physical intimacy in marriage is like icing on a cake. If the basic cake is mediocre, the icing won't be of great enjoyment.

Any couple who have a less-than-happy overall relationship will likely never have the fulfillment and joy of intimacy that a harmoniously married couple have. A couple who are fighting, launching verbal barbs back and forth, will never have the intimacy of a couple with a good overall relationship.

A key ingredient is kindness, which is a derivative of *agape* love. Depth of intimacy is built upon a spiritual foundation. That is *agape* love which manifests itself in genuine kindness one toward another.

The issues of life remain spiritual. A marriage built upon the foundation of *agape* love, *phileo* love, kindness, benevolence and trust will likely have the degree of sexual fulfillment for which the world continually strives but which it rarely realizes. God's way is always best.

SOUND ADVICE

"The wife hath not power of her own body, but the husband: and likewise also the husband hath not power of his own body, but the wife."—Vs. 4.

In this verse the apostle gives sound advice for couples. Both husband and wife ought to yield to the physical desires of each other in bed. The word translated *power* has the sense of authority or control. In other words, a wife has control or authority over her husband's body in physical intimacy; likewise, the husband has authority or control over his wife's body.

Modern "politically correct" ideology might view such a principle in terms of empowerment and choice. Rather, the Scripture is setting forth the principle of mutual consideration. It parallels the idea of giving of yourself for your loved one. Simply, if the husband is in the mood for intimacy and the wife is not, she should do as he desires; or if the wife is amorous and

her husband would rather go to sleep, he ought to fulfill her desire.

Conversely, if one's spouse doesn't feel well or is exhausted, he should be considerate and wait for another time. One should always be willing to give himself physically to his spouse.

As far as you are concerned, determine your body belongs to your spouse. Always be available and *willing* to be intimate with your spouse. Not only will you fulfill a marital duty, you will add a substantial ingredient for a marriage which is enchanting.

> Always be available and *willing* to be intimate with your spouse.

Years ago my wife and I promised each other that we would always be available and willing for intimacy whenever the other so desired. There have been few times over these twenty-five-plus years that that promise has not been fulfilled. The knowledge that each is *always* willing and available to the other for romance has kept the "honey" in our honeymoon for more than a quarter of a century.

GOD'S PLAN FOR FIDELITY

"Defraud ye not one the other, except it be with consent for a time, that ye may give yourselves to fasting and prayer; and come together again, that Satan tempt you not for your incontinency."—Vs. 5.

Paul uses a strong word at this point. The lexicon definition of *defraud* is to deprive someone of that which is rightfully his. The context is clearly of intimacy in the marriage relationship. To deny your spouse the privilege of physical intimacy is to deprive him of something which is rightfully his—that is, defraud him. The clear implication is that intimacy in marriage is not only normal and healthy, but is actually a *right*.

The exception to this principle is when both husband and wife *mutually* agree to abstain from intimacy for spiritual purposes. The word *consent* comes from the Greek word *sumphonos* from which our English word *symphony* is derived. The Bible says a couple ought to be steadfast in ongoing intimacy unless they are both in harmony on the matter of abstaining for a specific time.

In the Scripture, fasting is a voluntary denial of gratifying physical appetites for the purpose of humbling oneself before God and focusing altogether on the Lord through prayer. Usually it involves a partial or total abstinence from such simple things as food and drink.

This text says that fasting may also involve abstinence from physical intimacy with one's spouse. Such abstinence is to be only "for a time." The word used by Paul for *time* has the sense of a specific period of time. It is not an open-ended or indefinite period.

After the mutually agreed upon time, a couple ought to "come together again" physically. The reason for this is clear: "that Satan tempt you not for your *incontinency*." The word translated "incontinency" has the sense of weakness or a weak point. I frankly do not profess to understand how Satan as a spirit can perceive our weaknesses and seek to influence us through various temptations, but the Bible makes it clear that he can and he does.

The Devil came to Jesus in the wilderness after He had fasted for forty days, and sought to tempt Him to partake of bread. Satan knew after such a fast our Lord would be physically weak, and he sought to exploit that weakness. He failed.

Paul makes it clear that the Devil likewise can and will tempt a Christian morally when he or she is weak in that regard.

There is never any justification for infidelity; but when a spouse is deprived of natural and customary physical intimacy in the marriage bed, he or she is in a situation in which the Devil may well attack. The Bible says to defraud not one another in this matter.

In a tragic situation years ago a pastor-friend ruined his testimony and ministry. Though he had been married for some time, his marriage was rocky. I am not sure who was at fault in the day-to-day problems of their home, but he and his wife fought frequently. Because of the constant friction in the marriage, they had almost no physical intimacy. They continued like this for some time.

Meanwhile, another family in the church was undergoing marriage problems. The husband was inconsiderate of his wife and constantly abused her verbally. Both were emotionally immature. There was much fighting, bickering and ugliness in this marriage as well. Therefore, this couple also had virtually no physical intimacy.

She was quite attractive physically and was skilled in displaying her femininity. When she came to her pastor for counseling, she poured out her heart about how miserable it was at home. He foolishly counseled with her privately and on an ongoing basis. As he heard her sob about her miserable homelife, his heart went out to her. He had genuine compassion for the woman and felt sorry for her.

One day as he was counseling with her, he could not resist giving her a hug around the shoulders for encouragement. Because he had been so sympathetic and understanding concerning her troubles, she "loved" her pastor even more. When he put his arm around her to hug her, their "chemistry" clicked. She returned his modest hug around her shoulders with a passionate embrace and subsequent kiss.

Both were starved for intimacy, both knew better, but the embrace ignited a fire neither wanted to put out. Their desire was mutual. Several days later the pastor made an appointment to "counsel" the woman alone in her home while her husband was away. She was waiting for him. Their adultery ruined both of their marriages and deeply injured the church.

Both were one hundred percent wrong in their deed; but as I understand the Scriptures, Satan somehow was aware of their weakness and provided the temptation necessary for them to succumb.

I think of another sad situation. The woman fought constantly with her husband. Though she at times enjoyed intimacy with him, because of their incessant fighting, she would withhold herself from him as a means of getting even. Physical intimacy became almost nonexistent in their marriage.

The irony of it was, she desired physical intimacy with her husband; but because she was usually mad at him and trying to get even with him, she refused to participate. Satan somehow can spot such situations. He brought someone along at work who caught her eye. Her adultery became the strand which unraveled their marriage.

CONCLUSION

"But I speak this by permission, and not of commandment."— Vs. 6.

Paul concludes this section by pointing out that the instructions given in the first part of the chapter (that is, to marry and have ongoing intimacy) are good advice. However, they are not meant to be a commandment.

The greater lesson the Apostle Paul sets forth is the wisdom of healthy and regular physically intimate behavior in the marriage relationship. Not only is it a preventive of infidelity, but also it can surely be the icing on the cake of wonderful matrimony.

11.

AN EXPOSITION OF COLOSSIANS 3:4–19

Colossians 3 for the most part is not a chapter dealing directly with the husband and wife relationship. (The exception is verses 18 and 19.) However, the context clearly speaks of the relationship of the church to Jesus Christ. Inasmuch as the church is the bride of Christ and someday will be His wife, there is rich teaching on the relationship between the ideal Husband and His wife.

It would be well to recall that human marriage is a reflection of the ultimate marriage of Jesus Christ and His bride, the church. God has intended our marriages be patterned after that perfect example of His Son and His bride. Therefore, Scripture dealing with the relationship of Christ and the church provides an appropriate forum in which to study principles applying to human marriage.

The issues of life, particularly those pertaining to family and marriage, are intrinsically and fundamentally spiritual. Therefore, the spiritual principles found in Colossians are most apropos to the relationship between a husband and wife. Truly as these principles are integrated into a Christian marriage, they pave the way for a delightful, pleasant union paralleling the future union of Jesus Christ and the church.

As a pastor, I have observed that biblical Christianity is the key to a happy marriage. When both spouses are born again, spiritually mature, genuinely walking in the Spirit and manifesting the fruit of the Spirit, they have a relationship like unto the bliss the church and Jesus Christ will someday enjoy. Let's look at what the Holy Spirit through the apostle penned for us:

"When Christ, who is our life, shall appear, then shall ye also appear with him in glory.

"Mortify therefore your members which are upon the earth; fornication, uncleanness, inordinate affection, evil concupiscence, and covetousness, which is idolatry:

"For which things' sake the wrath of God cometh on the children of disobedience:

"In the which ye also walked some time, when ye lived in them.

"But now ye also put off all these; anger, wrath, malice, blasphemy, filthy communication out of your mouth.

"Lie not one to another, seeing that ye have put off the old man with his deeds;

"And have put on the new man, which is renewed in knowledge after the image of him that created him:

"Where there is neither Greek nor Jew, circumcision nor uncircumcision, Barbarian, Scythian, bond nor free: but Christ is all, and in all.

"Put on therefore, as the elect of God, holy and beloved, bowels of mercies, kindness, humbleness of mind, meekness, longsuffering;

"Forbearing one another, and forgiving one another, if any man have a quarrel against any: even as Christ forgave you, so also do ye.

"And above all these things put on charity, which is the bond of perfectness.

"And let the peace of God rule in your hearts, to the which also ye are called in one body; and be ye thankful.

"Let the word of Christ dwell in you richly in all wisdom; teaching and admonishing one another in psalms and hymns and spiritual songs, singing with grace in your hearts to the Lord.

"And whatsoever ye do in word or deed, do all in the name of the Lord Jesus, giving thanks to God and the Father by him.

"Wives, submit yourselves unto your own husbands, as it is fit in the Lord.

"Husbands, love your wives, and be not bitter against them."—
Col. 3:4–19.

Not all of this passage has direct application to the marriage relationship. Nevertheless, there remains a rich vein of
truth applicable to building a marriage paralleling Christ's
heavenly marriage.

Verse 4 establishes the context as being about Christ and
the church. Verse 5 begins with a "therefore," thus linking that
which follows to our relationship to Christ. Paul sets forth
several areas which will produce tranquillity in the home just
as surely as they will in the church. Let's look at them.

MORTIFY IMPURITY

*"Mortify therefore your members which are upon the earth; forni-
cation, uncleanness, inordinate affection, evil concupiscence, and covetousness, which is idolatry."*—Vs. 5.

The subject at hand is moral (or sexual) impurity. Just as
this is damaging to a church, it is destructive to a marriage.
Couples do survive immorality, but they do so with great
damage to their relationships.

A "glue" in a marriage is
trust. When people learn of
spouses' moral departure,
even if no other trouble
results, their trust in their
mates is shaken. Such cracks
in the foundations of marriages take years to repair and
are sometimes never repaired.

Moreover, there is more
to immorality than overt
adultery. A wife's catching

HEAVENLY
MARRIAGE

TRUST

MORAL IMPURITIES

her husband viewing pornography falls into the category of "uncleanness" mentioned in the text. "Inordinate affection, evil concupiscence, and covetousness" all fall into the broad category of "dirty sex."

I need not elaborate on the endless sewer of impure erotica abounding in Western culture. Such impurity is of course wrong, but it also sours the potential for a blissful relationship between husband and wife. Mark it down: moral impurity will take the honey out of a honeymoon. Therefore, flee any appearance of moral impropriety.

I think of a fellow who, though he initially did not enter into adultery, liked to flirt with whoever would accept it. It did not make much difference to him if his wife knew about it. On more than one occasion, he made lewd or suggestive remarks about the anatomy of other women to them. Such remarks eventually made it back to his wife. That couple certainly did not have a happy relationship. Impurity of any variety will sour the sweetness of a marriage.

"PUT OFF" THESE

"But now ye also put off all these; anger, wrath, malice, blasphemy, filthy communication out of your mouth.

"Lie not one to another, seeing that ye have put off the old man with his deeds."—Vss. 8, 9.

After giving warnings against all kinds of sexual immorality, this passage warns against what I call "garden-variety sin." Fortunately, most Christian couples will never have to deal with sexual immorality. However, virtually all spouses will have to deal with these everyday, ordinary problems which are an intrinsic part of human nature. These sins will take out of any marriage those things which are heavenly.

All of these are common to sinful human nature, and

every married person who has breathed has had to contend with these things. A person's being born again does not by itself rescind these problems. The new birth provides the *potential* to deal effectively with these problems. (We will detail that in a coming chapter.)

We are to "put off...*anger.*" On a colloquial level, we might use the more vernacular expressions, "being mad" or "losing our temper," in describing the idea of anger and wrath. The apostle uses the analogy of taking off soiled clothing. He says, "Put off all these." Being mad and/or losing our temper is as common as dirty clothes. The point, however, is to "put off" such sullied personality characteristics, even as we would soiled clothing.

Undeniably, our spouses will irritate us. Two people cannot live together in such close proximity as a husband and wife without irritating each other at times. However, spiritual maturity, which produces *agape* love, and mutual submission will squelch the urge to let our tempers "rip." Immature are those who run around being mad at their spouses.

Incidentally, only immature people remain mad. In the greater spectrum of a marriage relationship, being mad or losing your temper at your spouse is immature. Moreover, it most certainly will turn the sweetness of your relationship into vinegar. You will never have a marriage which is heaven on earth by allowing yourself the adolescent luxury of being mad or venting your temper.

In addition, we are commanded to "put off...*malice.*" Malice is holding animosity or ill will against another. It probably is a more intense form of being "mad." It is bitterness. Malice or bitterness manifests a lack of forgiveness.

Over the years I have had people say to me, "I will never forgive my spouse for what he [or she] did." Apart from being wrong-headed, such an attitude precludes resolving whatever conflict forms a barrier between marriage partners.

Malice will freeze out the warmth of relationship necessary to build a wonderful marriage.

Some years ago I heard of a wife who refused to forgive the indiscretions of her husband, though he had tried to apologize. Her bitterness toward her spouse put a chill on their marriage for years. Sadly, neither of them was a happy camper.

The word translated "blasphemy" is usually used in a theological sense, meaning "profaning the name of God or the things of God." In its more generic sense, it means "speaking in a derogatory fashion against another." Therefore, in day-to-day life, speaking in a disparaging way to or about another is a form of blasphemy.

If there is a sin which is present in *many* marriages, it is saying nasty things when a quarrel arises. Whether it is sarcasm, name-calling or some other form of verbal sharpness, verbal abuse is a form of blasphemy in its generic sense.

The Bible says, "Put off...*filthy communication.*" I am utterly amazed by how many Bible-believing, Christian people resort to profanity and other foul language when they get into a fight at home. Not only is it wrong, it will curdle the sweet cream which could have made a pleasant topping to your relationship. You will never have the pleasant harmony needed to build a wonderful relationship when you allow yourself the cheap thrill of a nasty tongue. Put it off like you would a soiled garment.

Then notice finally in this sequence the injunction to *"Lie not one to another."* Trust is a precious commodity in a marriage relationship. People usually enter into marriage with an assumed trust of their spouses. However, when that trust is shattered, it is a difficult and often long process to restore it. Once the dish is broken, it is not easy to glue it back together.

The word *infidelity* in a literal sense has nothing to do

with immorality. Rather, it literally means "untrustworthiness." To be sure, adultery will show a lack of trustworthiness, but lying will do the same thing.

I have known married people who would not think of committing adultery, but they certainly have been otherwise devious with regard to their mates. Hiding a purchase from a spouse or hiding some incident is devious; and such, together with lying, has put a crack in the stability of many a home. Frequently that crack is not sufficient to fracture the marriage altogether, but it certainly can take the joy out of a relationship. "Put off" lying and all forms of deviousness.

Verse 12 begins the other side of the coin. Whereas verses 5 through 9 dealt with unclean spiritual characteristics to be "put off" in our day-to-day relationships, verses 12 and following set forth items to be "put on." They are all spiritual.

"PUT ON" THESE

*"Put on therefore, as the elect of God, holy and beloved, bowels of mercies, kindness, humbleness of mind, meekness, longsuffering."—*Vs. 12.

In Christ, we are not only chosen (elect) but also holy and beloved. Therefore, we are enjoined to "put on" a number of spiritual virtues. Again the analogy of clothing is used. I personally enjoy putting on a clean shirt, fresh from the dryer. (When I was a boy, it was fresh from the

clothesline, which was even better.)

Just as a clean article of clothing is to be desired, each quality listed in verse 12 should be sought after because it is part of the recipe for a marriage which is heavenly. These qualities will abound in the marriage between Jesus Christ and the church in Glory, and they can be part of your marriage on earth in the meantime.

"Put on therefore...*bowels of mercies.*" This phrase is an idiom from biblical times. The Hebrew thought was that the seat of the tender emotions was the bowels. Indeed, deep empathy or compassion seems to well up from within us. In our modern Western culture, we might speak of someone's having a *heart* of compassion. The Hebrew mind would express the same idea as having *bowels* of compassion. The simple application is that we ought to be merciful and compassionate, certainly to our spouses. Both husband and wife are under such an injunction.

Some couples have little or no tenderness toward each other. I know such a couple. Though they have held together for years, how much happier and pleasant their relationship would be if they displayed "bowels of mercies" toward each other.

We come once more to *kindness*. Because so much has already been said about this word, we shall not belabor the idea again. The word used here is *chrestos*. This transliteration is only one letter different from that of the word *Christos*, the Greek word for *Christ*. This could help to remind us that to be Christlike is to be kind. Kindness is a necessary ingredient for a heavenly marriage. "Put on...kindness"!

Notice also the next quality, *humbleness of mind*. The thought is essentially of mental and emotional lowliness. Sometimes antonyms, expressing the opposite of an idea, are helpful in defining it. Humbleness of mind is the opposite of being proud, arrogant, opinionated and stubborn. Proud people tend to be prickly and difficult. In contrast, humility is a virtue which will lubricate the interaction of personalities. All things being equal, humbleness of mind will produce interpersonal tranquillity which is the foundation for happiness in a relationship.

Nowhere in the Bible is pride or stubbornness ever spoken of as desirable or virtuous. It always is set forth as sin and an evil to be avoided. The point to be made regarding marriage is that proud and stubborn people will never have the happiness and pleasantness of a couple possessing humbleness of mind. We are touching upon a hidden grace of life which truly is spiritual. It will prepare the way for pleasantness between spouses. Be willing to humble yourself unto your spouse. "Put on" humility!

The next quality listed is *meekness*. Again, because this virtue has been discussed in some detail in Chapter 9, we will make only brief comment on it here. It is a spiritual quality. It essentially is a self-discipline of emotion, attitude, temper and other reactions which produce an individual who is seemingly cool, calm and collected. Because meek individuals have their temper and emotions under control, they at times are perceived as timid or shy. Rather, true meekness is a solid sign of spiritual maturity. It evidences an individual whose spirit is in control of the rest of his or her being. It by no means is a weakness, but rather a silent strength.

Meekness of both parties in a marriage will preclude or control many a squabble. It is a spiritual virtue which tends to keep things on an even keel. It also is a spiritual referee within us controlling the impulse to shoot off our mouths or lose our tempers. True meekness will produce a serenity of rapport which is the foundation for happiness and true enjoyment. "Put on...meekness"!

Finally, in verse twelve, we are enjoined to "put on...*longsuffering*." The word in the Greek text has two nuances. On the one hand, it conveys the sense of being slow to avenge, which is quite similar to the idea of forbearance in verse 13. The other nuance is of patience in the sense of perseverance, steadfastness or constancy. Inasmuch as the next quality in verse 13 is forbearance, perhaps the latter sense is in view here. If that is so, perseverance certainly is a virtue in a marriage.

I have watched many a young wife run home to Mom and Dad whenever things became a little bumpy at her house. In my view, a spouse is better served to stay put and work out the problem than to run back home. Stick-to-itiveness is a virtue in most any forum. It certainly is so at home. I am of the opinion many a divorce could be avoided if one or both parties were just long-suffering. Ride out the storm. It will pass. Patience to bear with and ride out difficulties is indeed a virtue.

FORBEARANCE AND FORGIVENESS

"Forbearing one another, and forgiving one another, if any man have a quarrel against any: even as Christ forgave you, so also do ye."—Vs. 13.

To forbear one another is essentially to put up with each other. Even people who love each other will aggravate each other on occasion. But the Bible says to forbear one another. When we are weary or not feeling well, our threshold for tolerating irritation drops. (There is certainly a time each month when many a woman becomes very sensitive.) Little things may become burrs under the saddle. We become crabby.

It is good for us to realize our own foibles and to recognize times when our spouses are undergoing duress. A mark of maturity (spiritual and otherwise) is the ability to overlook the little things in our spouses which "bug" us. All things being equal, accept your spouse as he or she is. Realize few people have altogether similar backgrounds or habits of doing things. If the point of irritation is such you cannot overlook it, then sit down appropriately and 'speak the truth in love.' Talk about it. But in the final analysis, forbear one another. Have the grace and maturity to overlook little things your spouse does which bug you. Love your spouse for who he or she is.

You will find *your* level of happiness in your marriage will be higher by forbearing your spouse than by nit-picking about whatever happens to bother you at the moment. Give of yourself for your spouse in forbearing. You will add honey to your honeymoon.

"Forgiving one another...even as Christ forgave you, so also do ye." There is nothing your spouse has ever done which you cannot forgive. When we consider the magnitude of sin which Jesus Christ has forgiven in His mercy and grace,

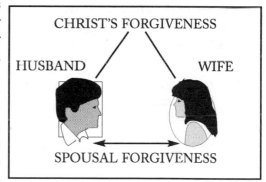

our problems pale in comparison. The Bible says to forgive even as Christ forgave us. When Jesus Christ saved us, He forgave a multitude of evils. So ought we to forgive. Of all people, this ought to include our spouses.

I am thinking of two couples who are separated by several states and whom I knew in different decades. In each marriage there was infidelity. In fact, in the first situation, the adultery was blatant. Yet the poor, wounded wife graciously forgave her wayward husband. He surely did not deserve her kindness, yet she bore with him. Thankfully, after several very difficult years, their marriage was restored to an even keel.

In the second case, the immorality was far less flagrant. In fact, as far as I know, it amounted to a one-night encounter. Yet the innocent wife refused to forgive her husband. She stubbornly hardened her heart against him. That marriage went downhill fast and never recovered.

More frequently the bone of contention between many a couple is less dramatic. It might be some financial misfortune or hurt feelings. But sadly, many an immature individual carries a grudge and harbors bitterness against a spouse for a long period of time. Not to forgive is adolescent, immature, shallow and cheap. It reveals a hard heart. When you will not forgive your spouse, you reveal there is something wrong with you which is as bad as whatever has offended you, and quite possibly worse. When you will not forgive, you will not have a heavenly marriage.

Forbear one another. Forgive one another.

AGAPE LOVE

"And above all these things put on charity, which is the bond of perfectness."—Vs. 14.

The Holy Spirit now comes to perhaps the most important article of clean spiritual clothing: "put on *charity*." As mentioned at length in an earlier chapter, the word *charity* in the Authorized Version is translated from the Greek word *agape*. It is the most basic word for *love* in the New Testament. The apostle says, *"Above all these things* put on charity" (love). Because an entire chapter was used to develop this idea, we will not embellish at any great length here. But it is significant, the Bible says, to put *agape* love above everything else in one's marriage. Give of yourself for your spouse endlessly.

Moreover, *agape* love is "the *bond of perfectness*." The concept underlying the word translated "perfectness" is of completion or fulfillment. In applying the idea to our person, it is maturity. A giving of oneself indeed is the essence of maturity. Such maturity tends toward perfecting a marriage.

We live in an age where there is much talk about fulfillment or of being fulfilled in life. God has a simple key to such fulfillment. It is called *agape* love. Selflessly give of yourself for your spouse. Not only will it reveal maturity on your part, it will also bond you ever more closely to your mate. Furthermore, *agape* love is the basic sugar which goes to develop the sweetness of a marriage which is heaven on earth. Once again, the key is spiritual.

THE PEACE OF GOD

"And let the peace of God rule in your hearts, to the which also ye are called in one body; and be ye thankful."—Vs. 15.

The Bible says to let that peace rule in our lives! The word translated "rule" has the sense of being an umpire. The peace of God emanating from fulfilling the spiritual principles mentioned above will become a spiritual "umpire." It will referee our emotions, our tongues, our attitudes, our dispositions and our reactions to those about us. When we allow the peace of God to control our being, it will in turn affect our relationships with those about us. In a marriage, that includes the relationship with one's spouse. Troubled water in a marriage is an advertisement that the peace of God is not ruling in that marriage. The reason is that even

more basic principles briefly outlined above are dysfunc-
tional. (Recall living by faith, the inflow of God's Word,
obedience to God, righteousness, and walking in the Spirit.)

Finally, in verse 15, notice the injunction to be *thankful*.
This is good for every area of life, but it certainly is good for
a marriage. Thank each other. To do less is an admission of
ingratitude and a taking for granted of the other. Thanking
your spouse for all the little things he or she does certainly
will add sweetness to your relationship.

Husband, thank your wife for the meals which she pre-
pares, for cleaning the house, for her kindness and thoughtfulness. Thank her for the good work she does with the children. Thank her for taking care of your clothes. Thank her
for her charms. Just be thankful to her.

Wife, thank your husband for his love, for providing for
the family, for the chores and maintenance he does around
the house. Thank him for his leadership. Thank him for loving you.

Now, I imagine some are thinking these things are the
duties *expected* in a marriage. Perhaps. But the point is, be
thankful to your spouse. Express your thanks verbally and otherwise. It will certainly preserve the honey in your honeymoon.

To be thankful is set forth as an imperative. We are commanded by God to be thankful. "Be ye thankful"!

WISDOM

"Let the word of Christ dwell in you richly in all wisdom."—
Vs. 16.

We touch here upon a principle which is profound to the
Christian experience and ultimately to our marriages as well.
The Word of Christ mentioned here is none other than the
Word of God. A marriage in which both parties are rooted

in the Word of God on a daily basis will already know most of the spiritual advice contained in this book. Such a marriage will probably already be a good marriage.

However, there seems to be an almost universal phenomenon when couples are having difficulty. In the course of counseling with such, I usually ask if *both* are in the Word of God daily in their individual lives. The answer is always the same: "No."

God's Word will solve a multitude of problems in our day-to-day lives, including problems in our marriages. However, it is even more effective in precluding or preventing problems. As we go to the Word of God each and every day, 365 days a year, and allow it to soak down into our hearts, it will change the way we live.

The vast majority of marriage problems are spiritual in nature. People live their lives ignoring scriptural principles and spiritual laws. They will inevitably have trouble. In a coming chapter, we will expand upon this principle more fully. But at this point, suffice it to say, "Let the word of Christ dwell in you richly."

Incidentally, the word "richly" has the sense of "abundantly." Make God's Word something that abounds in your life. It will provide the ongoing influence in your life which will lay the groundwork for a marriage which is heaven on earth.

Moreover, it will develop within you a godly wisdom which will enable you to make right decisions. As godly wisdom accrues in your life from the Word of God, you will bypass many, many problems and difficulties which erode the heavenly from your matrimony. "Let the word of Christ dwell in you richly in all wisdom"!

DO ALL FOR JESUS

"And whatsoever ye do in word or deed, do all in the name of the

Lord Jesus, giving thanks to God and the Father by him."—Vs. 17.

Whatever we do we ought to do in the name of the Lord Jesus. If everything we said and did in our marriages were done in the name of the Lord Jesus, we would eliminate most of our problems. If we would evaluate our attitudes, actions and assertions in light of the teaching, example and sacrifice of the Lord Jesus, we could have marriages which are heavenly.

THE SUBMISSION OF THE WIFE

"Wives, submit yourselves unto your own husbands, as it is fit in the Lord."—Vs. 18.

Inasmuch as this principle has been discussed at length in earlier chapters, we will not say a great deal more here. However, notice the phrase, "as it is fit in the Lord."

As evidenced in our earlier comments on this subject, it clearly is God's plan for the wife to be in submission to her husband. Perhaps the clearest example of this is none other than the appropriate submission of the church to her Bridegroom, Jesus Christ. As the ultimate example of a heavenly marriage, the church is in submission to Jesus Christ.

The word translated "fit" has the sense of "appropriate." Therefore, it is only appropriate, or fit, for wives to be in submission to their husbands. Again, it is a key for having divine happiness in a home.

THE LOVE OF THE HUSBAND

"Husbands, love your wives, and be not bitter against them."—Vs. 19.

As we have already discussed the submission of the wife

192

to her husband, so we have earlier detailed the love of the husband for his wife. Therefore, we will not comment further at any length on this principle. However, note the enjoinder, "and be not bitter against them." The thought is self-evident. Fellows, never allow yourselves to become bitter against your wives. They may not always do all they ought to do nor be all they ought to be. But love them and lance the ugly boil of bitterness as quickly as it appears, flushing away the poison thereof. Bitterness will produce sourness which will negate the sweetness of a marriage that could otherwise be heavenly in nature.

In summary, the Word of God lists a whole basketful of dirty items we need to "put off." This is incumbent upon us as Christians, married or single. However, if any would have a marriage relationship which is truly pleasant, these things must be given no place. "Put off" the ugly things, ranging from moral impurity to nastiness of spirit. We are enjoined to "put on" the clean and attractive wardrobe of the various virtues mentioned in this chapter.

SECTION IV

FINAL THOUGHTS

12.

THE FUNDAMENTAL PROBLEM AND GOD'S SOLUTION

A DEFECTIVE HUMAN NATURE

The root of most marriage trouble is spiritual. The bitter root goes far deeper than is readily evident. The Bible makes it clear our human nature has a major defect. In the New Testament Epistles, human nature is routinely called "the flesh." Though a term such as *the flesh* might seem to refer to the body, it in fact refers to the spiritual human nature with which all are born.

In a word, the Bible clearly teaches our human nature (the flesh) is corrupt. It is intrinsically selfish. Every human being upon the face of this planet possesses such a corrupt spiritual nature. It is the root cause for day-to-day troubles like bickering, sarcasm, lust, pride, arguing, hatred and hostility. In addition, it is the seat of loss of temper, greed, envy, violence, drunkenness, debauchery and all manner of sexual impurities. All of these are destructive to a home and will drain out of any marriage all that would be heavenly.

Envy, pride and stubbornness are rooted in the old spiritual nature, the flesh. So are an ugly temper, bitterness, refusal to forgive and a sharp tongue. They all gurgle up from the foul nature lying within our heart. A rebellious spirit which says, "No one is going to tell me what to do" also comes from the flesh, as does a desire for drunkenness or other intoxication. All these are spawned in the spiritual nature the Bible calls "the old man."

Any form of dishonesty or deviousness has its source in the old, sinful human nature—the flesh. The urge for base sexual gratification (be it adultery, fornication, pornography or a host of other deviant sexual behaviors) emanates from the corrupt human nature with which we were born. Nastiness, spiritual ugliness, being self-serving or foul-mouthed, deceitfulness, meanness, unthoughtfulness, pouting and inconsiderateness are a partial listing of the attributes of the flesh.

Every man or woman who has ever said "I do" at a marriage altar has entered into matrimony with just such a grotesque spiritual nature. Most people do not have any real understanding of their human nature, but it is present nonetheless. People's marriage problems stem from their defective spiritual nature. The secular world commonly refers to it as "human nature." The Bible calls it "the flesh."

As a couple launches out onto the sea of matrimony, usually before long one spouse upsets the other by some undesirable trait of his or her defective spirit. It may be by selfishness, stubbornness, loss of temper, a sharp tongue, a mean spirit, jealousy, rebellion, envy, sexual indiscretion or intoxication. Sooner or later (and usually sooner), one spouse will cross the other. Sparks fly, and often a simmering resentment or hurt feelings linger.

It is no wonder for many that marriage is not heaven on earth. The ultimate trouble is spiritual. If a couple is going to have the harmony ultimately producing a wonderful, warm, heavenly marriage, something must be done about the root cause for the source of these problems.

A SPIRITUAL NEW BIRTH

God's solution to the problem has been to create within us an entirely new human spirit (or nature). Throughout the New Testament, this transaction is called the new birth. In

John 3, the account is recorded of Nicodemus' coming to Jesus by night. Jesus' simple statement to Nicodemus was, "Except a man be born again, he cannot see the kingdom of God." Nicodemus went on to argue with Jesus about the feasibility of such. Jesus' reply was again simple: "Ye must be born again."

Those who receive Christ as Saviour are born again; they receive a spiritual nature from God which is of His holy and righteous character.

Specifically, it is the Holy Spirit who is most active in the new birth. Jesus explained to Nicodemus:

"Except a man be born of water and of the Spirit, he cannot enter into the kingdom of God.

"That which is born of the flesh is flesh; and that which is born of the Spirit is spirit."—John 3:5,6.

In the flow of the context, Jesus contrasted physical birth with spiritual birth. This new birth occurs when one receives and trusts Jesus Christ as his personal Saviour.

"But as many as received him, to them gave he power to become the sons of God, even to them that believe on his name:

"Which were born, not of blood, nor of the will of the flesh, nor of the will of man, but of God."—John 1:12,13.

When people receive Christ as personal Saviour, they are born again. That spiritual birth is not physical, nor does it involve human participation; rather, it is of God.

When God saved me, He created within me a new spiritual nature brought forth by the Holy Spirit. Today I, in effect, have two natures: the defective and perverse one with which I was born *and* the new spirit created within me by the Holy Spirit. The latter over the course of time has made a profound change in my life and, consequently, in my marriage.

This new birth has produced a new nature within me. Whereas my old, fallen nature was passed on to me from Adam and Eve, my new nature is born of God. It is *begotten of God* and therefore is a new creation within me. It is created in righteousness and true holiness.

SALVATION

Sin and its ally, the old nature, have not only fouled our hearts; they also have indicted us in judgment. In God's salvation, however, all of this is dealt with. Being saved is a broad spiritual transaction which includes being born again and receiving eternal life.

About three decades ago, I trusted Jesus Christ as my personal Saviour. That day, November 16, 1966, I was born again. I also was saved from going to Hell. It was the most important day in my life, and I have never for one minute regretted it. I never will.

That day I received a new spiritual nature which remains within my heart to this day. I have not always done all I ought to have done. I have not always been all I ought to have been. Yet since the Lord saved me, life has been more abundant than before. In addition, the new nature God has given me has formed the basis for a marriage which is celestial.

Let's pause for a few moments and explain exactly how to be saved (or how to make sure you are saved).

It is crucial you realize your lost condition. As noted above, the Bible says we all are guilty of sin. "For all have sinned, and come short of the glory of God" (Rom. 3:23). That guilt has brought us under the condemnation of a holy God. There is absolutely nothing we can ever do to merit God's forgiveness. We are lost. The word *damned* means we are hopelessly condemned because of our sin (Mark 16:16). A major step in being saved is realizing the judgment we face because of our sin.

It is likewise crucial that we realize what Jesus Christ did for us in dying on the cross. Romans 5:8 says, "But God commendeth his love toward us, in that, while we were yet sinners, Christ died for us." The Lord is a God of love who yearns to save us. In His love, He sent His Son, Jesus Christ, into this world so that we might live through Him.

When Jesus Christ went to the cross almost two thousand years ago, God laid on Him the iniquity of us all. All of our sin was laid upon Jesus Christ as He hung upon the cross that awful day. He died not only *with* our sin upon Him, but also *for* our sin. He paid the penalty of our sin in our place and in so doing made it possible for us to receive eternal life and the new birth accompanying it.

The key to God's salvation is turning to and trusting in Jesus Christ as one's personal Saviour. Over two hundred times in the New Testament, God has set forth salvation by faith. For example:

"For by grace are ye saved through faith; and that not of yourselves: it is the gift of God:

"Not of works, lest any man should boast."—Eph. 2:8, 9.

In John 6:47 Jesus said, "He that believeth on me hath everlasting life." A word that perhaps most clearly illustrates the biblical concept of faith is *trust*. Trusting Jesus Christ is totally relying upon Him. It is total dependence upon Him for our salvation.

Therefore, the faith needed for salvation is turning to and then totally depending (or relying) upon the resurrected Christ to save. This is the faith the Bible describes as necessary to receive salvation. In Romans 10:9 the apostle wrote, "That if thou shalt confess with thy mouth the Lord Jesus, and shalt believe in thine heart that God hath raised him from the dead, thou shalt be saved." Believing in one's heart is totally trusting Him.

Specifically, this can be done while praying a heartfelt prayer. Romans 10:13 says, "For whosoever shall call upon the name of the Lord shall be saved." Calling on the Lord from the bottom of one's heart for salvation is an act of faith. It is not only taking God at His Word; it is trusting and depending upon Him. The moment you place your trust in Jesus Christ, you will be born again and given eternal life. You will be saved.

If you are not sure exactly how to pray, you may follow the simple prayer below. Just repeating it verbatim is of no merit. However, if you from your heart trust Jesus Christ, you will be saved. If you would have Jesus Christ save you and give you a new birth, then pray from your heart this simple prayer:

Dear Lord Jesus, I know I am a sinner. I know You died to save me. Now will You please save me. Please give me eternal life and the new birth. I now trust You and receive You. In Your precious name. Amen.

If you prayed this prayer sincerely, trusting Jesus Christ, God heard. According to Romans 10:13, you are saved. You have been born again, and you are on your way to Heaven. You are now a new creature in Christ spiritually (II Cor. 5:17). You may not *feel* any different, but faith is independent of feelings.

Much could be written (and much has been written) as to all you should learn and do as a new Christian. Perhaps the most succinct advice I might give you now is to go wherever you obtained this book and ask for further counsel and spiritual help. In all likelihood, they can direct you. The coming chapter will likewise set forth foundational spiritual principles for the Christian life.

If you are unsure you have ever genuinely received Christ as your Saviour, then pray from your heart the simple prayer given above. God will hear, and you may rest assured you have made sure of your salvation.

Let us then return to the major theme of this book. A wonderful Christian marriage likened to heaven on earth begins with both partners' having the spiritual foundation of the new birth. This forms the foundation and *potential* for a truly blissful home. Notice, I used the word *potential*. Being saved or born again does not in itself guarantee a delightful relationship, but it is the foundation for it. Later in this chapter, we will study the specifics of realizing the sweet fruit of the new nature in our lives.

THE NEW NATURE

The Apostle Paul, in contrasting our old nature with the new, wrote in Ephesians 4:24: "And that ye put on the new man, which after God is created in righteousness and true holiness." As described in an earlier chapter, the apostle uses the analogy of putting on clothing. Now that we have a new nature, the Bible says to put it on. Unfortunately, most of the time many a Christian leaves his new nature hanging in the closet and runs around in the unclean spiritual garment of the old nature.

Notice how the Scripture describes our new nature. It has been "created in righteousness and true holiness." When we walk in this new nature or spirit, two spiritual forces will be operable in our lives: the first is *righteousness;* the other is *holiness.*

As described earlier, righteousness is doing what is right morally, spiritually, ethically and any other way. Genuine righteousness is not pragmatic. It is principled. It is doing right because it is right. The opposite of righteousness can easily be found in the dour comments made earlier about the flesh.

A word which is common in the New Testament

concerning the old nature is *lust;* for example, "Walk in the Spirit, and ye shall not fulfil the lust of the flesh" (Gal. 5:16). In our late-twentieth-century vernacular, the word *lust* usually conveys the idea of sexual lust, and that certainly is *one* sense of the word. However, the word used in the Greek New Testament at this point implies a far broader spectrum of thought. It essentially is a reference to any desires, wants, likes and wishes.

An important principle to remember is that our old nature operates on the basis of *want, like, desire* and even *lust.* My old nature runs around on the level of wanting this or liking that or desiring something else. Hence, when I am living in the flesh, my basis of decision-making is formed by what I want or like or don't like.

Another characteristic of the flesh is found in Galatians 5:24: "They that are Christ's have crucified the flesh with the affections and lusts." Notice the word *affections.* If translated in more contemporary English, it has the sense of our feelings. My old nature, in part, operates on the basis of how I feel about a certain thing. We all are familiar with the attitude, "I don't feel like doing it." Or if asked why one did something, he might reply, "I just felt like it."

However, my new nature operates on a totally different wavelength. Its basis of decision-making is formed by the simple questions, "Is it right? Is it appropriate? Ought I do it?" Decisions made upon the basis of righteousness are totally independent of what one happens to like, dislike or feel like. They have nothing to do with whether I happen to want a certain thing. Righteousness is exclusive of my feelings. It is based upon moral and ethical principle. Therefore, whereas my old nature may want or feel like doing something, the new nature operates on the basis of what is right. There are profound implications to that.

The new nature also has been "created in...*true holiness.*"

Holiness is absolute purity. It is the absence of wrong, sin or the corrupt. Therefore, the new nature operates on the level of not only what is right but also what is morally and ethically pure. As evidenced earlier, the flesh is prone to all manner of impurity, be it sexual impurity or impurity of spirit. The new nature, "created in...holiness," is the antithesis of this.

THE FRUIT OF THE SPIRIT

Galatians 5:22,23 details a cluster of sweet fruit developing from the new nature. As a person is born again and begins to grow in the Lord, he yields more and more to the new nature. As he does, the new nature begins to manifest in the believer's life a cluster of sweet spiritual fruit. This is what is scripturally and classically known as the fruit of the Spirit. It is the spiritual qualities which begin to develop in our lives as we walk in the new spirit which God has given us.

Nine different types of fruit are mentioned. Each of these derives from the new nature, and each will affect a marriage relationship. I would submit, these qualities are the stuff of which heavenly marriages are made. (Also, contrast this cluster of spiritual fruit with the ugly, corrupt and troublesome works of the flesh mentioned earlier.) A marriage built with this pleasing fruit will be sweet indeed. One laced with the works of the flesh will be unhappy indeed.

GALATIANS 5:22,23

"But the fruit of the Spirit is love, joy, peace, longsuffering, gentleness, goodness, faith,

"Meekness, temperance: against such there is no law."

First is *love*. As we have seen in other portions of this

book, love, particularly *agape* love, is perhaps the most basic foundation of a Christian marriage. Here we are again speaking of *agape* love. The crucial principle is that *agape* love emanates from the new nature. Because an entire chapter dealt with this principle, we will not further embellish it here.

However, if we would have this pure and most desirable of spiritual qualities welling up within us, it is incumbent upon us that (1) we have a new spiritual nature; (2) we be spiritually mature enough to bear fruit; and (3) we actually walk or live in the new nature. The avenue through which ongoing *agape* love will be developed in a marriage relationship is for both parties to live in the new nature.

Notice then *joy*, the next part of the cluster. Joy is a spiritual quality which is often misunderstood. It does not necessarily refer to laughter or the thrill of fun. It is not a surface quality; rather, it is an internal spiritual quality. It might be likened to the pleasant gladness of a person who has no worries. It is a sweet gladness within. An individual with the spiritual quality of joy will tend to influence others to have joy too.

Consider a marriage relationship where both husband and wife have seen their spiritual natures grow to the point that they each have joy. That joy will be magnified in their marital relationship as it flows from each to the other. That sweet quality of joy flows from the new nature which God's Spirit has created within us.

Then notice *peace*. As mentioned earlier, peace is the prerequisite to true happiness. We never will be truly happy until the peace of God reigns in our lives. Peace is inner tranquillity which expands harmony of relationships. It is the opposite of strife and anxiety.

If we would briefly recall the ugly works of the flesh, it should be evident any one of those can produce strife in personal relationships. This certainly is true in a marriage relationship. The fruit of the Spirit in peace, however, is just the opposite.

Tranquillity, harmony and happiness of relationships are natural by-products of spiritual peace. When both a husband and wife have grown spiritually to the point where righteousness of living produces peace, they indeed have the potential for great happiness; but such happiness ultimately derives from the new nature as they walk therein.

Then notice *long-suffering*. Some of the synonyms for this concept are *patience, forbearance* and *slowness in avenging wrongs*. As we grow spiritually to the point where we begin to produce the fruit of the Spirit in our lives, long-suffering will be a part of this pleasant cluster. As we are patient with our spouses, fights and strife will be diminished. As we develop forbearance, irritations and annoyances growing within us will virtually evaporate, along with bickering, arguing and hassles.

Contrast this with the hostility, stubbornness, bitterness, temper and anger which are so common to the flesh. What a difference! Instead of getting mad about something, we have the patience to forbear with it. Instead of losing our tempers, we patiently work out the problem. The spiritual "lubrication" smooths the inevitable friction when two personalities live together. From the flesh will come strife. From the Spirit comes long-suffering. Walking in the Spirit continually will produce the celestial harmony of a heavenly marriage.

Then there is *gentleness*. Gentleness, as the thought occurs in the original language, is closely akin to the quality of kindness. (We have examined this idea at some length earlier.) It emanates from the new nature. As we yield to that new spirit, part of its sweet yield in our lives will be a gentleness of temperament which is kind.

A colloquial synonym might be found in the word *nice*. Though this common little word is much overworked, we always appreciate it when someone is nice to us. Being nice

is inherent in gentleness. Instead of being nasty to our spouses as the flesh incites our emotions, the new nature moves us to be nice.

The flesh is rough; the spirit is gentle. The old nature is nasty; the new is nice. The old is mean; the new is kind. Take your pick. One or the other is going to rule the roost in your home. Again, this charming quality flows from the new nature. Put it on and wear it continually.

Next we come to *goodness*. Few concepts are more basic than that of being good. The lexicon definitions include "pleasant, agreeable, excellent, upright and honorable." Few compliments are more positive and all-encompassing than saying someone is good. To be called a good wife or a good husband is an honor indeed. To be called good regarding integrity and moral character is a compliment difficult to surpass.

Goodness is the antithesis of badness. As trite as that might sound, it remains true. None of the wrong and evil of the flesh could be called good. Goodness of nature brings to mind such virtues as purity, decency, kindness and benevolence. A couple who both exude genuine goodness are going to have a wonderful relationship. As we grow in the Lord spiritually, this wholesome fruit will develop in our lives and marriages.

Faith is next on our list. It is a direct synonym of *trust*.

Trust surely is an unseen "glue" which bonds a marriage together. It is related to faithfulness. Moreover, faithfulness as a spiritual quality derives from the new nature as one learns to yield to it. The issues of life are fundamentally spiritual!

Notice, then, *meekness*. As noted earlier in this book, meekness is a spiritual quality which produces mildness or gentleness of emotion. It emanates from self-control of our emotions. It is similar in nature to the next item on the list, temperance. However, meekness pertains more to the control of our internal attitudes and emotions, whereas temperance pertains to our initiatives and responses regarding outwardly visible activities.

The concept of meekness as mentioned in the Scripture speaks of an individual's having emotion, passion and temper under control. Composure is a related concept, particularly as it would pertain to our emotions and attitudes. Meekness is a quality of fairly developed spiritual maturity.

Having our emotions and attitudes under the control of the greater principle of righteousness is indeed maturity. Moreover, much of the trouble in which we find ourselves is caused by our reacting wrongly when irritated or crossed. It is so easy to become angry (which is of the flesh) when someone else crosses us. Meekness overrules the temptation to be angry. It is very easy to indulge in hurt feelings when offended (which again is a product of the flesh). Meekness likewise overrules such temptation and considers the slight as an oversight. It is very easy to wallow in bitterness and self-pity over some incident. Meekness, which is self-control of our emotions and attitudes, overrules and presents a righteous attitude. Because meekness reacts to negative incidents in a mild fashion, it is assumed by the world to be a character weakness, when in fact it is a great strength.

In blending this mature virtue into a marriage, negative emotions, lost temper and adolescent reactions are minimized, if not eliminated. When a husband and wife both possess the biblical quality of meekness, rich indeed will be their marriage; few will be their conflicts. It is a spiritual umpire with strong roots in righteousness and *agape* love. It will richly season a marriage with both.

Finally, we come to the principle of *temperance*. Few virtues in life are more profound. *Temperance* could be restated in the more contemporary thought of *self-discipline*.

On a practical level, the differential between the flesh and the spirit is self-discipline: The flesh *wants* to do a certain thing; the person yielded to the new man disciplines himself to do what is *right*. The old man pursues what he *feels like* doing; the person yielded to the new man disciplines himself to do *as he ought*. The flesh operates on the basis of *desires and feelings;* the man yielded to the Holy Spirit operates on the basis of a *self-discipline to be pure*. The spiritual practices necessary to walk in the Spirit are impelled by the self-discipline to do as one ought to do.

Now draw this principle into a marriage relationship. When a spouse is tempted to be nasty to his or her mate, the self-discipline to do what is right intervenes and chills the temptation. When a husband or wife is tempted to indulge in adultery or other sexual impurity, the self-discipline to be pure squashes the temptation. As an individual is tempted to deceive another, the self-discipline to do right emanating from a mature new nature overrides the wrong urge.

Conversely, the self-discipline of temperance will impel one to do right in any regard. It may be determining to do right by being thoughtful of, helpful to or thankful to your mate. It may be the self-discipline to be responsible or punctual. Whatever the situation, the self-discipline (temperance) to do what is right and pure can only add strength, stability and pleasantness to a marriage.

The ultimate solution to the spiritual problem we all

possess is yielding to the new nature created by the Holy Spirit within us. This new nature can preclude all of the corrupt works of the flesh in our lives and marriages. It in turn can produce a sweet cluster of fruit, bringing a pleasantness and tranquillity found otherwise only in Heaven. The new spirit within us can produce relationships which are celestial in nature because *it* is celestial in nature.

The foundation to it all is turning to and trusting in Jesus Christ as our personal Saviour.

HOW TO WALK IN THE SPIRIT

The apostle wrote in Galatians 5:16, "Walk in the Spirit, and ye shall not fulfil the lust of the flesh." In other words, if and as we walk in the new nature created within us by the Holy Spirit, we will not have to contend with the flesh and all its mess. This is *the* key to a wonderful, godly marriage which is like unto heaven on earth. Walk (or live) in the new man created within us at the new birth, and your marriage can become celestial.

Though many Christians have been taught about their new nature, some do not live therein consistently, and this is their problem. Many Christians do not *actually* walk in the Spirit most of the time. Their only alternative is to walk in the flesh. Hence, large percentages of born-again people go through day-to-day life carrying the burdens of having hurt feelings or of being mad, argumentative, stubborn, proud, easily provoked, self-directed, bitter, pouty or crabby. They at times succumb to temptations to be deceitful, immoral or vindictive. Needless to say, their marriages are often less than stellar.

After watching born-again people in Bible-believing churches for more than a quarter of a century, I am afraid that litany is all too true. Why is it so? Though they possess a new nature, much of the time they have not put it on. It is still hanging in the closet of their heart. They are not actually wearing that beautiful new spiritual garment, and they therefore are not walking in their new nature.

The analogy of "putting it on" is apropos. On several different occasions the Apostle Paul used this figure regarding our new nature (Eph. 4:24; Col. 3:10, 12). I do not believe it is a coincidence the Holy Ghost chose this analogy. We need to put on our new nature every single day even as we put on clean clothing. To fail to do so leaves only one alternative: to wear the foul garment of the old nature. Unless we take steps to do otherwise, we will begin any given day in the flesh.

How do we actually walk in the new man? How do we put on that beautiful new spiritual garment the Holy Ghost gave us at salvation?

1. **Crucify the flesh.** Galatians 5:24 says, "And they that are Christ's have crucified the flesh with the affections and lusts." To crucify is to put to death. In other words, we must crucify our flesh as necessary. This is something which must be dealt with in our lives. If my wife and I would walk in the Spirit, we each need to crucify our flesh as frequently as necessary. Certainly, at least daily!

How is that done? In this vein, Romans 6:11 says, "Likewise reckon ye also yourselves to be dead indeed unto sin, but alive unto God through Jesus Christ our Lord." The thought of "to reckon" found here essentially means to make up one's mind. Therefore, what the apostle is teaching is to make up our minds to be dead indeed unto sin. Each day we must make up our minds we are not going to allow the sinfulness of the flesh to control our lives.

Romans 6:12 goes on to say, "Let not sin therefore reign in your mortal body, that ye should obey it in the lusts thereof." The lusts or desires of our flesh will seek total reign in our lives. The very nature of the flesh is self-aggrandizing.

To crucify our flesh is to determine each day, *As far as I am concerned, the flesh is dead. I am not going to live therein today. I will not succumb to the desires of my old nature. I will not allow myself to make decisions of thought or deed based upon how I feel about a certain thing, nor will I make decisions based upon what I want or like. As far as I am concerned, the flesh is crucified.*

That surely is more easily said than done. Therefore, each day I enlist the help of the Holy Ghost dwelling within me. He dwells within my bosom and must "go along for the ride," so to speak, in any event. Therefore, each morning I pause in prayer and ask the Holy Spirit of God to help me to crucify my flesh and to walk in the Spirit that day. Indeed, there are days when I must seek the help of the Holy Spirit more than once in subduing the flesh within me.

2. **Put on the new man.** Within the closet of our heart hangs that righteous, pure, spiritual nature which the Holy Ghost created at our salvation. Again, the Bible says to put it on. In Ephesians 4:24, the apostle wrote, "And that ye put on the new man, which after God is created in righteousness and true holiness." He also wrote to the Colossians: "Put on the new man, which is renewed in knowledge after the image of him that created him" (3:10).

Each day as I spend time with the Lord in prayer, I ask the Holy Ghost to help me to live in the new nature. I pause and mentally determine that this day I shall walk in the new nature God has given. I frequently (though perhaps briefly) contemplate the various qualities of the new nature and ask the Holy Ghost to help me to exemplify those attributes on any given day. Similarly, I ask the Holy Spirit to help me to walk in righteousness, love, wisdom, purity, humility, honesty, kindness, selflessness, thoughtfulness and any other spiritual virtue the Holy Spirit reminds me of.

Both dying to self and putting on the new man are spiritual in nature. Spiritually, I shift gears from one to the other. The fact is, my old nature was accustomed to ruling the roost before I was born again. When I was a young Christian attempting to walk in the Spirit, my flesh constantly sought to reassert itself. Habits of a lifetime were being challenged, and long-established habits do not change easily. It has not been easy to learn to deal with my flesh daily and walk in the Spirit, but the Holy Spirit has been present to assist.

I am saying, it will not be easy to develop a pattern of consistently walking in the Spirit if you are not accustomed to doing so. It takes spiritual strength and determination.

As we have looked in some detail at Ephesians 4:24 and Colossians 3:10, we have skipped over advice which is pertinent to the subject at hand. The strength required is spiritual indeed. From where does that strength come? "Be renewed in the spirit of your mind" (Eph. 4:23). To the Colossians Paul wrote of being "renewed in knowledge after the image of him that created him."

We are renewed in the spirit of our minds by yielding to "the new man, which is renewed in *knowledge* after the image of him that created him"! Where do we find that knowledge? The Word of God! The strength and determination to walk in the Spirit will come largely from the renewal the Word of God brings to our lives each day.

In II Corinthians 4:16, the apostle wrote of the inward man's being renewed day by day. The basics of the Christian life are found in spending time in God's Word every single day. One will never walk in the Spirit apart from spending time in God's Word *daily*. It is so simple, and yet so many struggle with the flesh because they have never disciplined themselves to be in God's Word 365 days a year. Practically, time spent in God's Word will do more to keep us walking in the Spirit than any other one thing. The profundity of the principle is exceeded only by its simplicity.

When both husband and wife walk in the Spirit, their marriage will move from being like traveling a bumpy back road to resembling cruising down a smooth expressway. It will change from being something *endured* to being something *enjoyed*. It will transform itself from sour fruit to sweet fruit. It will ascend from resembling purgatory to resembling Heaven. The key is spiritual. The principles are found in God's Word.

If you are born again, you have the spiritual suit of the new nature hanging in the closet of your heart; but *you and your spouse* must put on that new man and walk therein from henceforth. Though the change is not easy, you will never regret it.

13.

PUTTING IT ALL TOGETHER

In the preceding twelve chapters, we have studied principles and Scripture passages relating to marriage. The essence of this book may be summarized in ten fairly succinct concepts:

✓**1. Marriage can be heaven on earth.** I know. My dear wife, Pam, and I have experienced twenty-five years of marriage which we believe has been a taste of Heaven on earth.

The Scripture clearly teaches that the church is the bride (in prospect) of Jesus Christ and someday will be united with Him forever. That will be a heavenly marriage in a very literal way. The spiritual principles which will define that marriage may in considerable measure be applied to human marriage today.

As I have written, I have attempted to portray life experiences not only of our own marriage but also of multitudes of others I have observed as a pastor. These experiences have been analyzed in light of the Scriptures.

✓**2. The issues of life are fundamentally spiritual.** God has created each of us as a trichotomy (body, soul and spirit). The internal controlling element of one's being is his spirit. It influences and directs his mind and emotions and, indirectly, his body. Therefore, one's spirit and the spiritual principles which govern it are the keys to happiness and fulfillment in life.

There probably is not a more basic human relationship than that of a husband and wife. Marriage is eminently a spiritual proposition. For a marriage to be strong, warm and happy, spiritual principles must be followed.

✓3. The principles for a happy marriage are found in the Scripture. The Bible is preeminently a Book of spiritual principles. Because the Holy Spirit of God inspired its writing through various human authors, the issues of life are unfolded in the spiritual truth contained therein. When we apply these principles to our lives and integrate them in our day-to-day living, the spiritual foundation for a genuinely happy marriage relationship is laid.

The essence of this entire book may be summed up in the following statement: The key to a marriage which is heaven on earth is for both husband and wife to practice genuine New Testament Christianity in their day-to-day living. Bible Christianity is exceedingly practical. When both spouses consistently and faithfully practice the principles of Christian living as detailed in the Bible, they are on their way to a celestial marriage. Real Christian living will produce real happiness!

✓4. Walk in the Spirit continually. The whole spectrum of Christian living finds its focal point in walking in the Spirit, as discussed in the preceding chapter. When both husband and wife *actually* live their day-to-day lives in the new nature, the resulting fruit of the Spirit will season their marriage with heavenly qualities. Walking in the Spirit is directly related to the degree of exposure one has to the Word of God and its related spiritual practices.

There are no shortcuts. There are no quick, easy steps. Only as a Christian couple invests the time and effort to be in God's Word day and night, infusing spiritual strength and influence into their spirits, will they walk in the Spirit. Not until then will the pleasant fruit of the Spirit characterize their day-to-day living. Specifically, this involves a number of spiritual building blocks, including the following:

✓**5. Immerse your marriage in the full spectrum of love.** Recall the three types of love:

a. *Agape* **love.** *Agape* love is a giving of oneself for the other. It is selfless, others-oriented. It does not focus on oneself but on the other person. It manifests itself in kindness, patience and maturity. *Agape* love is always active and never passive. People don't "fall" into *agape* love. It is something each must work at. It is intrinsically spiritual in nature.

b. *Phileo* **love.** *Phileo* love is a sharing of oneself with another. It is being a friend to your spouse. It is having fellowship one with another. It is enjoying the interests of the other and having an ongoing line of communication. The Bible instructs that it is the wife who is to seek her husband's interests, and not the other way around.

c. *Eros* **love.** *Eros* love is sexual love. It is delicately related to the first two types of love. When there is strong *agape* and *phileo* love in a marriage relationship, the *eros* love will be the icing on the cake. The deepest fulfillment of *eros* love is rooted in the more spiritual concepts of *agape* and *phileo* love.

✓**6. Frame your marriage in righteousness.** The work of righteousness is peace, and peace is the prerequisite of happiness. When a married couple always does right by each other in every area, trust, peace and happiness are in their home. Righteousness as a moral and ethical principle will bring great stability to a marriage. Conversely, acts and deeds of unrighteousness in a marriage will bring friction and distrust, souring the relationship.

✓**7. Stabilize your marriage by wise financial practices.** The handling of family finances, though seemingly neither spiritual nor romantic, can make or break the tranquillity of a marriage. It can make or break marital bliss. Honest, ordered, disciplined spending and saving can add a great deal of infrastructure to wedlock.

✓8. "Husbands, love your wives." Perhaps the premiere admonition of the New Testament given to husbands is simply to love their wives. *Agape* love can solve a multitude of difficulties and cover a host of transgressions. It is commanded, and it is a principle which is selfless by nature. Many a marriage problem could be solved by a husband's truly loving his wife. Doing so is eminently spiritual in nature. It derives from the new man and is part of the fruit of the Spirit.

✓9. "Wives, submit yourselves unto your own husbands." The premiere admonition in the New Testament for wives is to have a submissive *attitude* toward their husbands. The flip side of the coin is for wives to *allow* their husbands to be the leaders of their homes, not only in deed but perhaps more importantly, in spirit. A rebellious and defiant wife is living in the flesh. She will make everyone in the home, including herself, unhappy. When the husband loves his wife and the wife is in submission to her husband, major ingredients for a celestial marriage are in place.

✓10. Always season your relationship with kindness. Kindness is spiritual in nature, a derivative of *agape* love. Kindness will preclude and preempt verbal nastiness. It is thoughtful and considerate. It places the other person's concerns ahead of self-interest. It is a major ingredient in a magnificent marriage. It is wonderful that kindness is a simple thing and anyone is capable of manifesting it.

These ten concepts only briefly summarize what has been considered throughout this book. However, as these (and the rest of the spiritual principles contained herein) are woven into the habits and character of our lives, marriages which are heavenly will emerge.

For a complete list of books available from the Sword of the Lord, write to Sword of the Lord Publishers, P. O. Box 1099, Murfreesboro, Tennessee 37133.

(800) 251-4100
(615) 893-6700
FAX (615) 848-6943
www.swordofthelord.com